BRIGHT SHADOW

A PLAY OF DETECTION
IN THREE ACTS

by

J. B. PRIESTLEY

LONDON
SAMUEL FRENCH LIMITED

Copyright © 1950 by J.B. Priestley
All Rights Reserved

BRIGHT SHADOW is fully protected under the copyright laws of the British Commonwealth, including Canada, the United States of America, and all other countries of the Copyright Union. All rights, including professional and amateur stage productions, recitation, lecturing, public reading, motion picture, radio broadcasting, television and the rights of translation into foreign languages are strictly reserved.

ISBN 978-0-573-11648-3

www.samuelfrench.co.uk
www.samuelfrench.com

FOR AMATEUR PRODUCTION ENQUIRIES

UNITED KINGDOM AND WORLD
EXCLUDING NORTH AMERICA
plays@samuelfrench.co.uk
020 7255 4302/01

Each title is subject to availability from Samuel French, depending upon country of performance.

CAUTION: Professional and amateur producers are hereby warned that *BRIGHT SHADOW* is subject to a licensing fee. Publication of this play does not imply availability for performance. Both amateurs and professionals considering a production are strongly advised to apply to the appropriate agent before starting rehearsals, advertising, or booking a theatre. A licensing fee must be paid whether the title is presented for charity or gain and whether or not admission is charged.

The Professional Rights in this play are controlled by United Agents LLP, 12-26 Lexington St, Soho, London W1F 0LE.

No one shall make any changes in this title for the purpose of production. No part of this book may be reproduced, stored in a retrieval system, or transmitted in any form, by any means, now known or yet to be invented, including mechanical, electronic, photocopying, recording, videotaping, or otherwise, without the prior written permission of the publisher. No one shall upload this title, or part of this title, to any social media websites.

The right of J.B. Priestley to be identified as author of this work has been asserted in accordance with Section 77 of the Copyright, Designs and Patents Act 1988.

BRIGHT SHADOW

Produced by the Oldham Repertory Theatre Club at the Coliseum, Oldham, on April 3rd, 1950, with the following cast of characters:

(in the order of their appearance)

PAMELA FOTHERINGHAM	*Penelope Davis*
MAJOR GEORGE BUTTERSHAW	*Harry Lomax*
COLONEL PHILIP RISBOROUGH	*Charles Simon*
MRS PROBUS *(the housekeeper)*	*Ivy Collins*
LESLEY DEREHAM *(the Colonel's niece)*	*Pauline Yates*
PETER WARTON	*John Trevor*
IVOR KEMP	*Ken Marshall*
DOUGLAS BARROW	*Alan Foss*

SYNOPSIS OF SCENES.

The action of the play passes in the sitting-room of Colonel Risborough's house, Fenston Manor.

ACT I—A Wednesday afternoon in Autumn, 1946.

ACT II—Thursday evening.

ACT III—Friday evening.

BRIGHT SHADOW

ACT I

SCENE.—*The sitting-room of* COLONEL RISBOROUGH'S *old country house, Fenston Manor. A Wednesday afternoon in Autumn, 1946.*

The room is comfortable and shows obvious signs of being thoroughly lived-in. There is a broad window R. *overlooking the grounds. Across the corner up* R. *there is a door which leads to the hall, entrance, kitchen, etc. The fireplace is in the wall* L. *In the up* L. *corner above the fireplace there is a small staircase of which the last few steps can be seen. At the top of the stairs, there is a small landing and, out of sight of the audience, a door which can be locked. The staircase leads to the upper part of the house, bedrooms, etc., but there is also access to these rooms via the door up* R. *The ceiling is low and heavy. There are some fine old pieces of furniture and old family portraits hang on the walls. A large sideboard stands* C. *of the back wall, and there is a desk and chair at the window* R. *A comfortable settee stands* L.C. *with a small coffee table below it. Easy chairs stand* C. *and* R.C. *At night, the room is lit with big heavy standard lamps. The switches are above the door up* R. *There is a bell-push in the wall above the fireplace.*

(*See the Ground Plan and Photograph of the Scene.*)

When the CURTAIN *rises it is late afternoon. The window curtains are open and a late sunlight streams in. The fire is burning cheerfully, and the standard lamps have not yet been lit.* COLONEL PHILIP RISBOROUGH, MAJOR GEORGE BUTTERSHAW *and* PAMELA FOTHERINGHAM *are seated cosily around the fire. They have just finished tea. The* COLONEL *is seated on the settee at the* L. *end of it. He is in his seventies, a tall, beaky, fine-drawn type who is now old even for his years. He speaks slowly and carefully, and moves in the same fashion. He is dressed in old well-cut tweeds. The* MAJOR *is seated in the easy chair* C. *He is in his late sixties and, in marked contrast to the* COLONEL, *is a roly-poly type, carelessly dressed, with a rather foolish face and a bland manner. He smokes his pipe and has an unfinished whisky and soda on the* R. *edge of the coffee table.* PAMELA *is seated on the settee at the* R. *end of it. She is a widow in her thirties, and is a fairly handsome, smartish, town-and-country type, with a superficial assurance that covers something deeply uneasy and uncertain about her. She smokes a cigarette. There is silence for a few moments. The* COLONEL, *rather erect, is brooding, and the other two are lolling and smoking in one of those silences that come at the end of tea among people in the country, well acquainted with each other.*

PAMELA (*making an effort to overcome her lazy feeling*). What's the time? (*She glances at her wrist watch.*) Well after five. I must fly.

MAJOR (*lazily*). You rush about too much.

COLONEL (*mildly*). Everybody does now. No point in it.

MAJOR. No point at all.

PAMELA. It's all right for you chaps. And anyhow, if I hadn't done some rushing this afternoon, I couldn't have joined you for our nice cosy little tea.

MAJOR (*smiling*). Then we forgive you.

COLONEL. Certainly. And delighted to see you again, Pamela. Did you say you were staying at the Lodge some time now?

PAMELA. About a month, I hope, though the whole place is horribly leaky and draughty these days—it's winter in there already—and my new married couple that I brought down from town have already started to shake their fat heads and grumble.

COLONEL. Never cared for married couples. One of 'em's always a passenger.

PAMELA. I'd call both these two passengers if passengers didn't have such a wretched time of it nowadays. Still, there they are, and the woman can just manage one meal fit to offer company. No use asking you to come over and try it, I suppose?

(*As* PAMELA *says this, the* MAJOR *catches her eye without the* COLONEL *noticing, and shakes his head.*)

COLONEL (*with grave courtesy*). No, my dear. I think George here will tell you I'm not quite fit enough yet to go out.

PAMELA (*hastily*). No, of course not. Later, perhaps. And anyhow, I'll be dashing in from time to time—if you want me to.

COLONEL (*smiling*). Of course. Always delighted to see you, Pamela. Besides— (*his manner changes slightly but noticeably*) I think I forgot to tell you that I'm expecting Diana in a few days' time.

PAMELA (*startled*). Diana!

(*The* MAJOR *catches* PAMELA'S *eye again and nods meaningly at her.*)

COLONEL (*rather testily*). Yes, yes. Why not?

PAMELA (*hastily*). Yes—of course. I wasn't thinking. Lovely to see her again.

COLONEL (*slowly*). When is it, George? My memory's so bad. Next Tuesday, isn't it?

MAJOR (*with a hint of a humouring tone*). That's right, Philip. Tuesday more or less, I fancy. Day I've always been fond of—

ACT I] BRIGHT SHADOW 3

Tuesday. Always hated Mondays and Fridays—scratchy sort of days.
PAMELA (*following the* MAJOR'S *lead*). I think I like Wednesday least, though I've not the foggiest notion why.
COLONEL (*rising slowly ; gravely*). Excuse me, Pamela. And don't go. Talk to George. But I've just remembered I haven't spoken to Mrs Probus about Diana's room. Must have everything ready for her in good time.
MAJOR (*rising*). Don't trouble, old man. I can attend to it.
COLONEL (*rather testily*). Certainly not. My business. (*He moves above the settee, then to the door up* R.) Least I can do for the child.

(PAMELA *rises*.)

(*He stands by the door*.) But don't run away, Pamela—I shan't be long.

(*He exits slowly and carefully up* R. *The* MAJOR *and* PAMELA *stand watching him*.)

PAMELA (*lowering her voice ; urgently*). So he's just the same.
MAJOR (*easily*). Yes. Always will be now, I think.
PAMELA. Lord—I nearly dropped an awful brick. But I'd forgotten for the moment—and when he said so calmly he was expecting Diana—I nearly jumped out of my skin.
MAJOR. My fault—I ought to have warned you he was still the same.
PAMELA. I don't know how you can bear it. I couldn't.
MAJOR. Let's sit down, shall we ?
PAMELA (*indecisively*). I really ought to be going.
MAJOR. Don't unless you really must. He'll remember asking you to stay—and he might worry if he finds you've slipped away.
PAMELA. I see. Well, it's the least I can do, I suppose. (*She sits on the settee at the* L. *end of it*.)

(*The* MAJOR *sits in the easy chair* C. *and re-lights his pipe*.)

But as I was saying—I don't know how you bear it. I know I couldn't.
MAJOR. He's an old friend, you know, and gives me a home here —and it's not much to ask in return—just to help him to keep his illusion going. You and I have probably a few illusions too that we'd like one or two people to help us cherish.
PAMELA. I have. One of 'em is that poor Wilfred was still in love with me when he got himself killed. But I'm not sure you've many little illusions, Major Buttershaw. Having a good look at you all over again, I suspect there's more in you than used to meet my eye.
MAJOR (*smiling*). I doubt it. You're flattering me—and very nice, too. But—going back to the Colonel—you must remember

too that I'm a medical man of sorts—old R.A.M.C. wallah, y'know —so I keep a kind of professional eye on him.

PAMELA. What about that wretched woman in the kitchen— Mrs Probus—who was devoted to Di ?

MAJOR. Yes, she takes it badly. Often comes to me in tears and threatens to leave, but I manage to jolly her along somehow. And young Lesley helps.

PAMELA. Ah—yes—there's little Lesley. I'd forgotten about her.

MAJOR. Good girl that. Don't know her well, do you ?

PAMELA. No, not had a chance. Remember, I haven't been round here much since Di's death—and it was after that that Lesley settled here. Not quite my type, I'm afraid. And I'm certainly not hers—remembering some of the cracks she took at me last time I was around. Not got herself engaged or anything yet, I suppose ?

MAJOR (*with a twinkle*). Doesn't get much of a chance, poor kid. But I fancy she has a high standard—my influence probably.

PAMELA. Ten to one she'll end up with five children on a ruined poultry farm in North Wales. It's a pity she wouldn't do for . . . (*She breaks off and rises.*) No, that's idiotic— (*she moves restlessly to the fireplace, looks at and touches the ornaments on the mantelpiece*) I'm forgetting. (*She moves restlessly to the sideboard up* C. *and again looks at and touches things on it.*)

MAJOR (*mildly*). Stop flitting about.

PAMELA (*moving to the writing table* R.). I can't help it. You shouldn't have made me stay. (*She fidgets with the pens.*) Suddenly —now—I feel all churned up.

MAJOR. Well, take it easy. And what's idiotic—and what are you forgetting ?

PAMELA (*turning*). Do you know who's coming to stay with me tomorrow ?

MAJOR. No. Are you changing the subject ?

PAMELA. Not really. (*She moves above the easy chair* R.C.) You'll see. (*Rather defiantly.*) Ivor Kemp is coming.

MAJOR (*gravely*). That's not a good idea, is it ?

PAMELA. Oh—I suppose not. But I ran into him in town, and he seemed rather miserable, and he can be so amusing at times— and I felt sorry for him and thought how bored I'd be down here. And why isn't it a good idea ? What does it matter now ? I'll keep him away from the Colonel, of course. And Douglas Barrow is still away, isn't he ?

MAJOR. o, he isn't.

PAMELA (*aghast*). Are you sure ?

MAJOR (*rising*). I caught sight of him in Longbridge only two days ago. (*He picks up his drink from the coffee table, moves to the fireplace, stands with his back to it and drinks, emptying his glass.*)

PAMELA. Oh, Lord ! I told poor Ivor I was certain Douglas was still abroad somewhere. Still—we shall be ten miles apart—

and I'll just have to be careful about asking people who invite us anywhere, if Douglas is going to be there. How did Douglas look?
MAJOR. As if he was drinking at least as hard as ever. (*He looks at his empty glass.*) And, incidentally, so am I. (*He moves to the sideboard.*) Join me?
PAMELA. No, thanks, it's too soon after tea. Where do you chaps get all your booze from?
MAJOR (*pouring out a whisky and soda for himself*). Fellow who runs the wine and spirit department of the brewery at Longbridge used to be our Quartermaster. Besides, nobody here except me does any serious drinking.
PAMELA (*lightly*). But you're quite the little rumpot, aren't you?
MAJOR. Yes, but it keeps me good-tempered. There's another type, who should never be allowed to touch it, who get angry when they drink.
PAMELA. Like Douglas Barrow, for instance.
MAJOR. Quite so. (*He drinks.*)
PAMELA (*after a pause ; suddenly*). I wish I hadn't come down now. I don't like this. I thought this wretched Diana business was all done with.
MAJOR (*moving to the fireplace*). Well, isn't it?
PAMELA (*easing down* C.). Somehow it doesn't feel like it. The Colonel still talking about her as if she was alive—giving me the creeps. And I'm here again—and I've gone and asked Ivor Kemp to stay—and Douglas is back again. I don't like it. I don't like it at all.
MAJOR. It's a mere coincidence.
PAMELA. I don't like coincidences of this sort. I'm not sure I believe in them either.
MAJOR (*coolly*). And I'm not sure I do.
PAMELA (*half humorously, half seriously*). You're a comfort, aren't you?
MAJOR. I try to be. Take it easy. And if you've got something on your conscience, try to forget it. (*He drinks.*)
PAMELA (*eyeing the* MAJOR). What do you mean—something on my conscience?
MAJOR. I don't know.
PAMELA (*sharply*). I should think not.

(MRS PROBUS *enters noisily up* R. *She is an elderly woman, once a childrens' nurse and now a housekeeper. She is a rather vague, worrying woman, with a slight country accent. At this moment she is extremely worried, almost in tears. She carries a large tray.* PAMELA, *startled, turns quickly.*)

MAJOR. Where's the Colonel, Mrs Probus?
MRS PROBUS (*agitatedly*). Gone up to her room himself— (*she moves to* R. *of the settee*) and talking about having a fire lit in there—he would go, and nothing I could say would stop him. I know how

it is with the Colonel—and I'm as sorry for him as you are, Major Buttershaw—but I tell you, I can't stand much more of it.

MAJOR. All right—I'll attend to him. (*He drinks, emptying his glass.*) He oughtn't to be up there by himself—it's dangerous. (*He puts his glass on the coffee table and moves up* L.)

MRS PROBUS. I daresay—but I couldn't stop him. You know what he is.

MAJOR. I'll bring him down. Shan't be a minute, Mrs Fotheringham.

(*He exits up* L. PAMELA *stands and watches* MRS PROBUS, *who moves to the coffee table and begins, rather slowly, to put the tea things on the tray.*)

PAMELA (*quietly*). I must say I don't blame you, Mrs Probus. He gave me a shock—talking about Diana coming here next week. I nearly dropped a very nasty brick.

MRS PROBUS (*stopping her business with the tea things*). Well, what do you think it's like for me—who brought her up since she was a baby—felt about her as if she was my own?

PAMELA. Yes, of course. We all know that.

MRS PROBUS (*almost tearfully*). It's like somebody digging up a grave—not letting the poor thing rest at last.

PAMELA (*breaking* R.). Oh—for God's sake . . .

MRS PROBUS (*looking steadily at* PAMELA). There's no need to start talking like that, Miss Pamela—I mean, Mrs Fotheringham.

PAMELA (*turning; hastily and apologetically*). I know—I'm sorry. Something upset me, too. I wish Colonel Risborough would come down—and then I could say good-bye and go.

MRS PROBUS (*resuming her work with the tea things*). He'll come down if the Major tells him he ought to. That's how it is here now, though you mightn't think it. (*She straightens up, looks at* PAMELA *and lowers her voice.*) Looks like nobody much round here, doesn't he, with his soft pussy way and his pipe and his whiskies?

PAMELA (*confidentially*). You mean—the Major?

MRS PROBUS (*confidentially*). Yes. Looks just like a hanger-on, so to speak, doesn't he? But don't make no mistake about that one.

PAMELA (*moving to* R. *of* MRS PROBUS ; *softly*). You sound as if you don't like the Major very much.

MRS PROBUS (*sourly*). I don't know as I like anybody very much any more. And half my time I feel as if I'm walking about in a miserable dream that I can't get out of.

PAMELA (*with a rather false cheerfulness*). Now—Mrs Probus—it isn't as bad as that.

MRS PROBUS (*looking at* PAMELA). Perhaps not, Mrs Fotheringham. But if you'll excuse me—and, after all, I've known you since you were a little girl—I wouldn't say you were feeling so good neither, these days.

(PAMELA *reacts, but tries to pass it off.*)

PAMELA (*crossing below* MRS PROBUS *to the fireplace*). Probably not. But then—who is ?

(LESLEY DEREHAM, *the* COLONEL'S *niece, enters up* R. *She is an attractive girl in her early twenties, with something open and direct about her, in sharp contrast to the other characters we have so far met. Her manner is genuinely cheerful. She wears outdoor walking clothes, with a bright scarf around her neck.*)

LESLEY (*moving* C.). Oh—hello, Mrs Fotheringham.
PAMELA. Hello, Lesley. How are you ?
LESLEY. I'm fine, thank you.
MRS PROBUS (*moving with the loaded tray above the settee*). This tea's finished long since.
LESLEY (*looking at the tray*). It doesn't matter, thanks. I don't want any. (*She takes two scones from the tray.*) I'll just take two of these. (*She eats the scones during the next few speeches.*)

(MRS PROBUS *exits with the tray up* R.)

PAMELA. You seem rather gay.
LESLEY (*easing down* C.). I feel rather gay—somehow.
PAMELA. Any particular reason ?
LESLEY. No. But you know the way sometimes you feel that everything's all right really.
PAMELA. That sounds like a young man to me.
LESLEY (*irritated*). Well, it isn't. And I don't see why it has to be.
PAMELA. It usually is.
LESLEY. Well, this time it isn't. As a matter of fact I've just walked four or five miles by myself, and haven't spoken to a soul—except to exchange the usual good afternoons.
PAMELA. Don't you find it boring here just with two old men ?
LESLEY. Yes, often.
PAMELA. I couldn't endure a week of it.
LESLEY (*dryly*). No, I don't suppose you could.
PAMELA (*imitating a cat*). Miauw !
LESLEY. No, it isn't miauw at all. I wasn't being catty—I was just stating a fact. Where's uncle Philip ? You've seen him, haven't you ?
PAMELA. Yes, we had tea together. Then he went off to see that Diana's room would be ready for her next Tuesday.
LESLEY (*calmly*). Yes, he still won't admit to himself that she's dead. The Major says he never will now—that it's a definite fixed thing he must accept. About everything else he's quite sane—though of course he forgets easily—and rather sweet really.
PAMELA (*staring at* LESLEY). I must say—you take it very calmly.
LESLEY. Well, why not ?
PAMELA (*uneasily*). I couldn't. In fact, I can't.
LESLEY. But why shouldn't you ? After all, he's an old man—

who was always a bit eccentric, so we were always told in the family—and Diana was his only daughter—and he absolutely worshipped her. And it was all rather a nasty mess. So it's not surprising really.

PAMELA (*uneasily and hastily*). Oh—it's easy for you to talk, Lesley. You didn't know Diana as some of us did. You weren't mixed up in that horrible business—you weren't even here when it happened. You can't begin to understand.

LESLEY (*coolly*). All right, then, I can't. Let's talk about something else.

PAMELA (*more to herself than to* LESLEY). I was a dam' fool to come down here again—but my flat's upside down with the builders and I can't leave the Lodge here empty too long. And now I've gone and asked Ivor Kemp to stay—and Douglas Barrow's back. And, listening to the Colonel, you'd think at any moment Diana would be walking into the room.

LESLEY. Would you mind very much if she did?

PAMELA (*annoyed*). Di was one of my oldest and very dearest friends.

LESLEY. Yes, I know. (*She turns her back to* PAMELA, *starts to hum, removes her scarf and places it on the desk.*)

(PAMELA, *still annoyed, stares at* LESLEY *for a few moments, then crosses to* R.C.)

PAMELA (*sharply*). What did you mean, then, by asking me if I'd mind very much if Di did come walking into the room?

LESLEY (*turning ; somewhat surprised*). Because you sounded as if you didn't like the idea at all. And yet—as you say—she *was* one of your oldest and dearest friends.

PAMELA (*on edge ; harshly*). But she's dead, isn't she?

LESLEY. Yes.

PAMELA (*irritably*). Well, let's say that I don't like the idea of somebody who's dead walking into the room. (*She breaks impatiently to the sideboard.*) Will that do? (*She takes a cigarette from the box on the sideboard, and lights it.*)

LESLEY. I don't want to argue about it—but as you've asked me—well, no, it won't do. You see, if Diana was dead, then she couldn't walk into the room. If she could walk into the room, then she couldn't be dead—and you'd have one of your oldest and dearest friends restored to you.

PAMELA (*moving to the fireplace ; airily*). All of which, my dear, sounds quite pointless to me.

LESLEY (*easing* R.C.). All right, then. It's pointless.

PAMELA (*after a pause*). But you don't think it is, do you?

LESLEY (*coolly*). No, and neither do you.

(*There is a short pause as they look at each other, then the* COLONEL *and the* MAJOR *enter up* L. *They look at ease and are smiling. The* MAJOR *eases up* C.)

COLONEL (*moving to* R. *of the settee*). My dear Pamela, you must forgive me. But Lesley's been entertaining you.
PAMELA. Oh—yes—very nicely.
COLONEL. Good ! Well, let me offer you something to drink—a glass of sherry perhaps—eh ?
PAMELA. Thank you, Colonel. But can I have something rather strong—with plenty of gin in it ?
COLONEL. Ah—George here is the man for that sort of thing.
MAJOR (*turning to the sideboard*). I am. What you want is the *Buttershaw Benefactor*—an old and well-tried remedy. (*He mixes a drink for* PAMELA *and a whisky and soda for himself.*)
PAMELA. Remedy for what ?
MAJOR (*over his shoulder*). Oh—for boredom—irritation—bad nerves.
COLONEL. What about you, Lesley ?
LESLEY. Not now, thank you, Uncle. (*She switches on the lights by the switches above the door up* R., *then draws the curtains.*)
COLONEL. Not for me either, George. Well, let's sit down and be comfortable. (*He sits on the settee at the* R. *end of it.*)
PAMELA (*sitting on the settee*, L. *of the* COLONEL). I ought to be miles away by this time—but I suppose it doesn't matter—only the Frasers.

(LESLEY *sits in the easy chair*, R.C.)

COLONEL. Ah—how is Fraser ?
PAMELA. I don't know. I was going to find out—but now there won't be time. However, they'll keep.
LESLEY. I saw Dorothy Fraser out with the dogs this afternoon.
PAMELA. I hate doggy women.
MAJOR (*moving with the drink for* PAMELA *to* L. *of the settee*). You try this—and you won't hate anybody. (*He gives the drink to* PAMELA, *then returns to the sideboard for his own.*)
PAMELA (*taking the glass*). Thanks. (*She looks at it, then raises the glass.*) Well—cheers everybody. (*She takes a small drink and is impressed.*) Good Lord ! What did you put in it ?
COLONEL (*chuckling*). Don't ask. They're an old secret of George's. We used to say he slipped in something from his medicine chest. Didn't we, George ?
MAJOR (*easing* C.). And I did too, sometimes. But not this time. (*He drinks.*)
LESLEY (*severely*). You drink far too much.
COLONEL. He always did. Didn't you, George ?
MAJOR (*coolly*). Yes, always. But I can hold it.
COLONEL. Perfectly true. Always could, too.
PAMELA (*after a sip of her drink*). Three of these and I'd be screaming drunk.
LESLEY (*interested*). Try it and see.
PAMELA (*hastily*). No fear !

COLONEL (*politely*). I've probably asked you this already—I've a wretched memory these days—but how do you find the Lodge now?

PAMELA. Going to ruin at full speed—and with most of last winter still lurking in it. Both the drawing-room and the dining-room are hopeless—I'll have to live in the breakfast-room. And I'm expecting a guest tomorrow . . .

(*She breaks off sharply as the* MAJOR *gives her a warning look.*)

COLONEL. A guest, eh? Anybody we know?

PAMELA (*with an assumed casual air*). No, just somebody I ran across in town. (*She sips her drink.*)

COLONEL. When Diana arrives, we'll give a little dinner party—perhaps next Wednesday or Thursday.

MAJOR (*with assumed heartiness*). Good idea, Philip!

LESLEY (*with assumed heartiness*). Lovely!

COLONEL. Mind you, if we can manage it, we ought to try and keep her quiet for a few days. You know the kind of life she leads—racketing round. Just high spirits, of course, though I keep telling her she can easily overdo it. Eh, Pamela?

PAMELA (*with an obvious effort*). Oh—yes—of course. I—couldn't agree more.

(*There is an awkward pause, which is broken by* MRS PROBUS, *who enters up* R.)

MRS PROBUS. Please—sir . . .

COLONEL (*turning*). What is it, Mrs Probus?

MRS PROBUS. Huskins is here, sir.

COLONEL (*impatiently*). Well, put him in my study—and tell him I'll see him shortly.

MRS PROBUS. Yes, sir. But there's also a—a young man called to see you. Wants to have a talk with you.

COLONEL. Possibly. But do I want to have a talk to him?—that's the point. Who is he?

MRS PROBUS (*easing* R.C.; *lowering her voice*). Says he used to come here one time during the war—and I think I can remember him coming—one of those young Air Force chaps we used to have here.

COLONEL. Ah—that's different. Glad to see one of those youngsters again. Take his hat and coat—and then show him in.

MRS PROBUS (*moving to the door up* R.). Yes, sir.

COLONEL (*hastily*). Oh—and ask him his name—it'll save me the trouble—and then announce him—you understand?

(MRS PROBUS *nods and exits up* R. *The others stir and turn expectantly towards the door up* R. *The* MAJOR *finishes his drink, puts his glass on the sideboard, and moves to the fireplace.* PAMELA *puts her glass on the coffee table. The* COLONEL *is obviously pleased by this visit.*)

ACT I]   BRIGHT SHADOW   11

(*He lowers his voice a little.*) Fine lot of boys they were—and it's very pleasant to know that at least one of 'em's still alive—and hasn't forgotten us. Ought to ask him to dinner—if he can stay. May have come to live in the neighbourhood, of course. If not—and he can stay a day or two—we ought to offer to put him up. However, we'll see.

(MRS PROBUS *enters up* R.)

MRS PROBUS (*announcing*). Mr Peter Warton, sir.

(PETER WARTON *enters up* R. *He is an attractive fellow in his thirties. Quite apart from his heavy tan, he has the look of a man who has been living far away from England, something about the loose cut of his clothes, for example. Normally, one feels, he would have an assured and independent air, but this particular moment is ticklish and so he is a trifle nervous and hesitant. He speaks good English without any suggestion of any class and social background, very much a contemporary type, without any " good public school manner". He clearly belongs to a different social order and world from those of the* COLONEL. *Once he gets going, his manner is easier and more attractive than his actual speeches suggest. He is more pointed in talk than he is in manner. He has the air of a man who has knocked about a lot and can rely on himself. He is not shy, but obviously he keeps a good deal of himself in reserve. The* COLONEL *rises.* MRS PROBUS *exits up* R.)

PETER (*moving* C.). I'm sorry to call on you like this, Colonel Risborough.

COLONEL (*meeting* PETER *at* C.). Not at all, Mr Warton. Delighted to see you. (*He looks closely at* PETER.) My memory's not too good, these days, but I think I remember you now.

PETER. I didn't expect you would, because I was only here a few times—in nineteen forty-two it was—and I was a flying-officer then at the bombing station near Dillingley. Several of us used to come over.

COLONEL. Of course you did. And very jolly evenings we had, too. Of course, my daughter arranged it all, and unfortunately she's not here at present, although I'm expecting her back in a few days.

PETER (*puzzled*). It was Miss *Diana* Risborough we used to meet here ?

(LESLEY *rises.*)

COLONEL. Naturally. Only daughter I've got—Diana.
PETER (*puzzled*). But . . .
LESLEY (*interrupting ; firmly*). Won't you have a drink, Mr Warton ?
PETER (*turning to* LESLEY). Oh—hello !
LESLEY (*smiling*). Hello !
PAMELA (*curiously*). Do you two know each other ?

LESLEY (*hurriedly*). No—Mr Warton asked me the way, that's all.
PAMELA (*archly*). Now I understand about this feeling gay.
LESLEY (*hurriedly*). Don't be ridiculous.
COLONEL (*fussily*). Now what's all this ? My fault, I suppose. Should have introduced you at once instead of talking about Diana. (*He eases above the settee and introduces* PAMELA.) Mr Warton—Mrs Fotheringham, a neighbour and an old friend of my daughter's.
PAMELA (*smiling*). How d'you do. Y'know, I believe we met here once.
(PETER *merely nods and smiles*.)
COLONEL (*indicating* LESLEY). This is my niece—Miss Lesley Dereham. Not here when you used to visit us.
LESLEY (*smiling*). In the WRENS in those days. Hello again.
PETER (*gravely*). Hello again.
COLONEL (*turning towards the* MAJOR). And this is my old friend and brother officer of India and the first war—Major Buttershaw.
PETER. How do you do, sir.
MAJOR. How do you do. And what about that drink now ?
COLONEL. Yes—yes—of course.
PETER. Well . . .
MAJOR (*moving to the sideboard*). Join me in a whisky ?
PETER. All right, thank you—whisky.
COLONEL. Good ! Not settled in this neighbourhood, have you ?
(*The* MAJOR *pours out a whisky and soda for* PETER, *and re-fills his own glass*.)
PETER. No, sir. Haven't settled anywhere in this country. I went to Burma after I left here, during the war, and now I'm out there helping to run a transport company.
LESLEY (*eagerly*). Is that fun ?
PETER. Sometimes it's fun, sometimes it isn't. (*To the* COLONEL.) No, I came down here—well—specially to see you, Colonel Risborough.
PAMELA. Where are you staying ? (*She picks up her glass, finishes her drink, then replaces the glass on the coffee table*.)
PETER. Didn't particularly intend to stay, but I've left a bag at the *Fenston Arms*.
COLONEL. *Fenston Arms !* My dear boy, we can't allow you to stay there—horrible place. Besides, my daughter . . .
MAJOR (*turning quickly from the sideboard and interrupting ; firmly*). Philip, what about Huskins ? He's waiting. Shall I . . . ?
COLONEL. No, of course not. You can't deal with Huskins—don't know his language. (*To* PETER.) Gardener—handyman chap. Always have a talk to him about this time. I'll go and get rid of him. (*He moves slowly to the door up* R. *Over his shoulder*.) Can't allow this *Fenston Arms* nonsense, y'know. Out of the question.
PAMELA (*rising ; loudly*). Now I really must go. (*She moves to* L. *of* PETER.)

COLONEL (*stopping and turning*). Oh—must you, Pamela ?
PAMELA. Definitely. (*She holds out her hand to* PETER. *With a seductive smile.*) Good-bye, Mr Warton. Come and see me—Fenston Lodge, only a mile away—if you do stay on. (*She shakes hands with* PETER.) Love to see you. Give me a ring. Good-bye, Major. (*She moves to the door up* R.)
MAJOR. Good-bye.
PAMELA. 'Bye, Lesley darling.
LESLEY. Good-bye.
COLONEL (*opening the door up* R. *for* PAMELA). I'll see you out Pamela—and then attend to Huskins.

(*He slowly and ceremoniously ushers* PAMELA *off up* R., *then follows her out. The* MAJOR *hands* PETER *a drink, then picks up his own glass and moves below the settee.*)

PETER (*taking the drink*). Thanks. (*He raises his glass.*) Well—cheers ! (*He drinks.*)
MAJOR. Cheers ! (*He drinks.*)
LESLEY (*sitting in the easy chair* R.C.). I propose we sit down.
MAJOR. And talk. (*He sits on the settee.*)
LESLEY (*gravely*). And talk.

(PETER *sits in the easy chair* C. *There is a pause.*)

PETER. Well—who starts ?
LESLEY. Was it just politeness—your calling here ?
PETER. No.
LESLEY. I didn't think it was.
PETER. I've had other things to do, of course, mostly connected with my business out there—but still, you might say I've come several thousand miles to call here.
LESLEY (*deeply sorry*). Oh—then you came to see Diana.
PETER. No, I didn't.
MAJOR (*quietly*). She's dead, you know.
PETER. That's what I was told.
MAJOR (*quietly*). She died nearly three years ago.
PETER. I know. But her father . . . ?
MAJOR. He's old, and not too well-balanced. She was his only child and he worshipped her. The shock was too much for him.
PETER. So that's it.
MAJOR. We have to humour him. There's nothing else to do. If we tried to force him to realize the truth—it might be dangerous. I'm an old medical man, by the way.
LESLEY. Well—I'm not . . .
PETER (*with dry humour*). No, I didn't think you were.
LESLEY (*not rudely*). Shut up ! (*To the* MAJOR.) But I've never been sure you're right, you know.
MAJOR (*with quiet firmness*). Take my word for it, Lesley. I

know what I'm talking about. And don't forget I've known your uncle for over forty years.

LESLEY. All right. (*To* PETER.) And now you can tell us why you came all this long way, just to call here, when you knew Diana was dead.

MAJOR. That's a bit brutal, Lesley.

LESLEY. I didn't mean it to be. But I believe it's best to be frank—to speak your mind—tell the truth.

PETER (*with a hint of challenge*). You do—do you?

LESLEY (*with a touch of defiance*). Yes, I do.

PETER. Good! So do I.

LESLEY. But you haven't answered my question.

PETER (*carefully*). I came here to see if I could talk to her father about her.

MAJOR. Well, you can't, you know. I hope I've made that clear.

PETER. Yes, that's clear enough.

MAJOR. I'm sorry.

PETER. So am I.

LESLEY. Look—I don't understand this.

MAJOR. It's perfectly simple, my dear. Correct me if I'm wrong, Mr Warton.

PETER (*a trifle grimly*). Go ahead.

MAJOR. I wasn't here at the time, but I gather that Diana used to entertain little groups of Air Force fellows here. Mr Warton was one of them. He and his friends were very grateful to Diana, probably half in love with her. He learns that she's dead. So he calls here to offer his sympathy to the Colonel—to tell him what a wonderful girl they all thought she was—and how sorry they all were. And a very nice gesture, too.

LESLEY (*to* PETER). Is that all it was?

PETER. No.

LESLEY (*nodding*). I thought not.

MAJOR. You mean—I'm wrong?

PETER. No. Your account's all right as far as it goes. But it doesn't go far enough.

LESLEY. Sorry, but I'm going to say it again. I thought not.

PETER. And why did you think not?

LESLEY. It sounded too sentimental for somebody like you.

PETER. You may be right. I wouldn't know. But if it's my turn to be frank—speak out—tell the truth, I'd say that what brought me here was a kind of curiosity. (*He pauses and looks at them.*) You don't like the sound of that, do you?

MAJOR. Candidly—no.

PETER (*to* LESLEY; *rather grimly*). And what about you—who wanted to see all the cards on the table?

LESLEY. I say no, too.

PETER (*grimly*). I thought you would. Well, so much for being frank—telling the truth. Not taken us very far, has it?

ACT I] BRIGHT SHADOW 15

LESLEY (*hotly*). Oh—don't be stupid. Diana was my cousin. Colonel Risborough is my uncle—and now he's heartbroken—and not—not quite sane—and it's tragic. I wasn't here when it happened—and I've never understood why it's all so hush-hush and so many people seem to be odd and uncomfortable about it all. But it's the limit when you—a stranger—just come poking your nose in. If curiosity brought you here, then I think the sooner you go, the better.

MAJOR. And though I wouldn't put it quite as strong as that—well, I agree.

(PETER, *who has taken all this quite coolly, nods and rises. Then he looks down at them.*)

PETER. Right. (*He puts his glass on the coffee table.*) Well, I was about to push off anyhow, because, if I can't talk to Colonel Risborough, then obviously there's no point in my staying. But you might as well let me finish what I was going to say. I said that what brought me here was a *kind of curiosity*. But it's not the kind you mean—just a sort of nosey inquisitiveness into other people's private affairs. It's something quite different. It's—well—wondering what kind of world this is—what people are really like—what goes on below the surface of things. I don't pretend to know a lot, except about aviation and transport, but I'd like to know a bit more. I seem to have spent the last ten years in a kind of huge madhouse—up in the air, down on the ground—here in England, out there in the East—and whenever I have a chance, I feel I'd like to try and make some sense out of at least a few pieces of it.

LESLEY (*gravely*). I understand that. I've often felt like that myself. But where does poor Diana come into this?

PETER. She's one of the pieces. Because what happened to her doesn't make sense to me—it just makes everything look more senseless and idiotic than ever. Look at it from my point of view. There's a girl here—Diana Risborough. She asks us over here—plays, sings, dances, clowns around with the chaps, who are all half-barmy over her. She's beautiful, gay, young—and seems to have everything. We leave here, go off to Burma, can't forget her—and think to ourselves—there was somebody who had it all—Diana Risborough. For a lot of us she seemed to represent the best of everything we'd had to leave behind. Like a sort of princess. Can you understand that?

MAJOR. Yes, my boy. I can remember feeling just like that myself once—a long time ago.

PETER (*to* LESLEY). And you?

LESLEY. I'm a girl—and Diana was my cousin—I'd known her all my life—but—yes, I think I can understand.

PETER. Right. Now keep on looking at it from my point of view. About two years ago I ran into an ex-Raf type I knew in a club, and after we'd had a few *John Collinses* he said to me, " You were at that

Dillingley station one time, weren't you? Remember that girl—Diana Risborough? Pity about her, wasn't it? Oh—didn't you hear? Got married, made a mess of it, couldn't make a go of it with some other bloke, and finally did herself in. It was all hushed up a bit and smoothed over—you know—and they all pretended she'd had an accident with some sleeping tablets—the usual thing—but it stuck out a mile that she'd made a mess of it all round—and felt she ought to take the jump." (*He pauses and looks at them.*) That's more or less what I heard, several thousand miles away, and none of it seemed to make sense to me. It just made everything look more wobbly and nightmarish than it did before. I felt I had to know more about it. And that's why I came here.

LESLEY. Were you in love with her?
PETER. No.
LESLEY. I think you were.
PETER. Then you're wrong.
MAJOR. No, it doesn't follow, Lesley. I know what Mr Warton means now by his curiosity, though I gave it up as a bad job long ago myself. (*To* PETER.) But I still think you ought to go, y'know.
PETER. All right. I *am* going.
MAJOR. On the other hand, I think before you do go, you're entitled to know everything I can tell you about Diana.
LESLEY. Yes, of course, but you'll have to hurry up. Uncle may be back any moment now. (*She rises.*) He doesn't usually spend much time with Huskins. (*She moves to the door up* R.) I'll go and see what's happening.

(*She exits hurriedly up* R. *There is a short pause.*)

MAJOR. It's up to me to give you the facts, Warton, because Lesley wasn't here at the time, and of course it's impossible to discuss it with Colonel Risborough, whose mind is now a blank on the whole subject.
PETER. Doesn't he even remember she was married?
MAJOR. No. To him Diana's still the girl who entertained you fellows here. And she's always away, of course, but always about to come back in a few days. It's a mental defence mechanism really, I suppose. He can't face her death and so he's had to blot out everything that led up to it. Incidentally, he's never been a very stable type—and Diana was much the same. Lesley's very different, of course. Sound as a bell. Fine girl.
PETER. Yes—I like the look of . . .

(*He breaks off as* LESLEY *enters hurriedly up* R.)

LESLEY (*breathlessly*). I peeped into the study—and he's asleep. Huskins must have gone long since. Still, you'd better hurry up with your explaining.
MAJOR. Are you sure you want to hear this, Lesley?

LESLEY (*moving down* R.C.). Yes. I'm not sure I understand it all myself yet. And certain things keep happening . . .
MAJOR. What things?
LESLEY. No, go on. There isn't much time.
MAJOR (*to* PETER; *carefully*). Diana married a man called Douglas Barrow, a gentleman-farmer who lives about ten miles from here. Why she married him I can't imagine. But then I'm a bachelor and I've never really understood why anybody ever married.
LESLEY. Don't waste time talking rubbish. Diana married Douglas Barrow—and nobody understood why, because he's an unattractive bad-tempered man who drinks a lot.
PETER. Is that a fair description of him?
MAJOR. Yes. And the marriage didn't work. She accused him of being mean, suspicious, vindictive and cruel. He accused her of being extravagant, frivolous, and unfaithful to him. He also said afterwards—though not publicly—that she was a thief, that when she left him she stole several hundred pounds that didn't even belong to him.
LESLEY. I don't believe that, you know. It doesn't sound like Diana at all.
MAJOR. Barrow said that a man called Ivor Kemp had been her lover for some time. This is the man she went to when she left Barrow. But she and Kemp had a quarrel of some sort. She left him, in the middle of the night, to drive back here. She'd had some drinks. She ran the car into a ditch about a mile from here, and gave herself some cuts and bruises and perhaps a touch of concussion. We got her back here and put her to bed. She wouldn't talk. The following night she took a large overdose of barbiturates, and was found dead next morning. There was an inquest, at which I gave evidence.
PETER. What was the verdict?
MAJOR (*rising*). Misadventure. Accidental death. (*He puts his glass on the coffee table, then stands with his back to the fireplace.*) It can easily happen, you know, particularly if anybody has been in the habit of taking strong sleeping tablets. You take a strong dose—then you think you haven't taken any—so you take some more.
PETER. And do you think it happened like that?
MAJOR (*after a pause*). No. I think she committed suicide. And I imagine other people who knew her think so, too. And that explains what Lesley here was complaining about—I mean the whole business being so hush-hush and so many people appearing to be odd and uncomfortable about it all.
LESLEY (*a trifle dubiously*). Yes, I suppose that's it.
PETER. Is it?
LESLEY (*taken aback*). Well—isn't it?
PETER. I don't know. I'm just listening.
MAJOR. And all you're listening to, I'm afraid, is a rather sordid messy little story. Shocking, too, to anybody who knew her before

her marriage, as you did. But those are the facts. (*He turns and presses the bell-push.*)
LESLEY. Why are you ringing ?
MAJOR (*turning ; smiling*). I'm ringing for Mrs Probus—to ask her to bring Mr Warton's hat and coat.
LESLEY (*dismayed*). Oh !
PETER (*softly*). You agreed I ought to go—remember ?
LESLEY (*uncomfortably*). Yes, of course. (*She breaks down* R.)

(*There is a short pause, then* MRS PROBUS *enters up* R.)

MAJOR. Oh—Mrs Probus—would you please bring this gentleman's hat and coat. And try not to disturb the Colonel if you put them just outside the study.
MRS PROBUS. Oh—very well, sir.

(*She exits up* R.)

MAJOR. You see, I thought if we were finding your hat and coat out there, and talking, we might disturb the Colonel—and that might be awkward, as you can imagine. We must humour him.
PETER. Certainly.
MAJOR (*with a gesture towards the sideboard*). One for the road ?
PETER. No, thanks.
MAJOR (*picking up his glass*). Then I'll have it for you. (*He moves to the sideboard and pours out a whisky and soda for himself.*)
LESLEY (*turning abruptly and moving in to* R. *of* PETER). Well—are you satisfied ?
PETER. No, of course not.
MAJOR (*over his shoulder*). I'm sorry. But I've given you the facts.
PETER. Not the ones I want.

(LESLEY *looks startled, but before she or the* MAJOR *can reply*, MRS PROBUS *enters up* R. *She carries* PETER'S *hat and raincoat. She closes the door behind her and moves up* R.C. LESLEY *eases* R.)

(*He moves to* MRS PROBUS.) Thanks, Mrs Probus. (*He takes his raincoat from her, and slips it on.*)
MRS PROBUS. Was you one o' them Air Force boys that used to come here ?
PETER. Yes.
MRS PROBUS. It was very different then—very different.
PETER (*softly*). You'd known Diana a long time—hadn't you ?

(*The* MAJOR *picks up his drink and moves to the fireplace.*)

MRS PROBUS. Known her since she was a little baby—brought her up, you might say.
PETER (*softly*). What sort of a girl was she, Mrs Probus ? (*He takes his hat from her.*)

MRS PROBUS (*eagerly and half-tearfully*). She was the gentlest, sweetest, kindest-hearted creature there ever was—was Miss Diana. Couldn't ever have done no harm to anybody—and always in such wonderful spirits—laughing an' singing an' going on—but all in fun—an' never a bit of real harm in her. I miss her every minute—an' many a time I've wished to God they'd taken me to the churchyard the day they took her. (*She starts to cry.*) Oh—my little love—my dearie.

LESLEY (*moving quickly to* MRS PROBUS). Don't please—Mrs Probus—we all feel the same. (*She tries to comfort her.*) There—there.

MRS PROBUS (*recovering herself*). It's all right, miss. It was just him asking that.

(*She turns and exits hurriedly up* R.)

LESLEY (*glaring at* PETER). That wasn't very clever of you, was it?

PETER. No. And I'm sorry. I don't think I *am* very clever. But— (*he looks meaningly from* LESLEY *to the* MAJOR) I'm not such a fool as to imagine that I've learnt anything yet.

LESLEY. About Diana?

PETER. Yes.

MAJOR (*easily*). You've learnt everything I can tell you, my dear fellow.

LESLEY (*easing down* R.C.). What is it you want to know?

PETER (*at* C.; *quietly*). I want to know what it was that took her from the top of the world down to a suicide's grave. I want to know if Mrs Probus was right about her, or her husband was right about her. Was she unfaithful to him or wasn't she? Was this other fellow—Kemp—her lover, and, if so, what happened when she went to him? Why did she leave him and come back here? Why did she commit suicide—if she *did* commit suicide? What sort of woman was she? Was she what we thought she was, or what her old nanny thought she was, or what her husband thought she was, or somebody quite different? I told you I wanted to make some sense out of one little piece of life, perhaps because the way her death was reported to me out there, gave me a shock and I began brooding over it. All right—it's no dam' business of mine—I can't talk to her father, the man I came to see—you want me to clear out—and you're quite right so I'm going. Right. But don't imagine you've settled anything for me. I'm leaving with more questions than I came with. But—thank you, all the same. (*He moves to the* MAJOR *and holds out his hand.*) Good-bye. And thanks for the little story.

MAJOR (*shaking hands with* PETER; *amiably*). Not at all, my dear fellow. Sorry I couldn't do more for you. Good-bye.

PETER (*turning and moving to* LESLEY). Well—good-bye—Miss . . . (*He holds out his hand.*) Sorry, I've gone and forgotten your name now.

LESLEY (*not taking* PETER's *hand*). Dereham. Lesley Dereham.

And yours is Peter Warton. (*With a half-humorous ferocity.*) And you *are* a nuisance.
PETER (*genuinely astonished*). Why?
LESLEY. Because you barge in—from Malay or somewhere.
PETER. Burma—Burma.
LESLEY. What does it matter? But you begin asking questions and making mysterious remarks—and get me all excited and mixed up about poor Diana and a lot of other people—and then calmly hold your hand out and say good-bye as if you'd just dropped in to tea or something.

(PETER *laughs with genuine amusement.*)

(*Annoyed.*) All right—laugh. But it's not funny. And I *was* going to say I was sorry you're going, but now I'm not—I'm glad.
PETER (*half serious, but with a smile*). And I was going to say I was glad I was going, but now I'm not—I'm sorry.

(*As he holds out his hand again, the* COLONEL *enters up* R. *He carries a small suitcase.* LESLEY, PETER *and the* MAJOR *look at him in surprise.*)

COLONEL. I sent Huskins down to the *Fenston Arms* for your suitcase, Mr—er—Warton. And here it is. (*He places the case against the wall* R. *of the sideboard.*) Can't have you staying there, you know. (*He moves to* R. *of the settee.*) Eh, George?
MAJOR (*moving below the coffee table*). Well, I gather it's not—er—very convenient for Mr Warton to stay here.
COLONEL. Nonsense, nonsense! Perfectly convenient. Understood from the first—eh, Mr Warton?
PETER (*demurely*). I shall be very glad to stay, Colonel Risborough, if you don't think I'll be a nuisance.
COLONEL. Of course not. Take that coat off, my dear fellow. And Lesley, my dear, you might like to give Mrs Probus a hand with Mr Warton's room—or perhaps attend to it yourself.
LESLEY (*happily*). Yes, of course, Uncle.

(*She flashes a look of mischief at* PETER, *hurries to the door up* R., *and exits.* PETER *removes his raincoat and places it with his hat on top of the suitcase. The* MAJOR *moves to the fireplace.*)

COLONEL (*sitting on the settee*). You won't find it very lively here, I'm afraid, not until my daughter arrives—she'll brighten the place up, of course. I have to retire early, immediately after dinner, and Major Buttershaw usually comes up to my room and we play bezique. But my niece, Lesley, can invite some local people in to meet you, if necessary. I think you met Mrs Fotheringham, didn't you? Quite a lively girl in her way—and an old friend of my daughter's—and there are some other people, eh, George?
MAJOR (*dubiously*). Yes, Philip. Possibly.

COLONEL. We old fellows lose the habit of sociability—so long as we've one crony to yarn away with. But I expect you're wondering how Diana is these days, eh ?
PETER. Yes. I meant to ask you that.
MAJOR (*interrupting ; firmly*). Philip, I'll have to drag you away a minute or two—to the study, if Warton'll excuse us. (*He puts his glass on the coffee table and moves to the door up* R.) Something you ought to sign.
PETER. Of course.
COLONEL (*rising slowly*). You're getting fussier every day, George, 'pon my word you are. (*He moves to the door up* R.) Help yourself to a drink, my boy. We shan't be long.

(*The* COLONEL *and the* MAJOR *exit up* R. *As soon as they have gone,* PETER *looks around then moves to the desk, finds the telephone directory and starts to look through it. After a few moments, the door up* R. *opens and* LESLEY *peeps in. She sees* PETER *is alone, enters quickly and moves* C. PETER *turns to her*.)

LESLEY (*in a breathless whisper*). I want to tell you this, while I have a chance.

(PETER *moves to* R. *of* LESLEY.)

Pamela Fotheringham, that woman who was here, is having Ivor Kemp to stay with her tomorrow. And Douglas Barrow, who's been away for ages, has just come back. They were all mixed up with Diana and now they're all back here again. And I'm certain Pamela Fotheringham knows something that she's never told anybody—and she's frightened, too.
PETER. Thanks. And I want to tell you this. Your uncle has suggested that you invite some local people in to pass the long evenings, but the only ones I want to see are Douglas Barrow, Ivor Kemp and Mrs Fotheringham. I've been trying to find them in the telephone book.
LESLEY (*moving up* L.). I must fly. We can talk after dinner.
PETER (*moving to the sideboard*). Good !
LESLEY (*stopping and turning*). But you were in love with her, you know. Probably still are.
PETER. I'm not. But don't let's waste time arguing that point.
LESLEY. All right. But why are you bothering about her ?
PETER. I told you why.
LESLEY. Yes, but I don't believe all that stuff about pieces of life not making sense.
PETER. Why not ?
LESLEY. It doesn't sound like you. I feel you got it out of a book—or something.
PETER. But what do you know about me ?
LESLEY. Only what I can guess. But it's probably more than you'll ever find out about poor Diana.

PETER (*grimly*). Well, we'll see.

They stare at one another for a moment, then voices are heard off R. LESLEY *nods, turns and exits quickly up* L. *The* COLONEL *and the* MAJOR *enter up* R. PETER *turns to meet them with a smile as—*

the CURTAIN *falls quickly.*

ACT II

SCENE.—*The same. The following evening.*

When the CURTAIN *rises, it is after dinner, and coffee is set on the coffee table. The curtains are closed, the fire is burning cheerfully and some of the lights are on, so that the room looks warm and cosy. The* COLONEL *is seated on the settee at the* R. *end of it.* PETER *stands with his back to the fire. He holds a small coffee cup and saucer. They are looking hard at each other, and they hold this for a moment or two.*

PETER (*after a pause ; quietly*). Try again, sir.
COLONEL. No, my boy. Very good of you to bother. But I'm sorry—can't remember at all.

(PETER *moves to* L. *of the coffee table, puts his cup and saucer down on it, then tackles the* COLONEL *again. He speaks very distinctly and slowly, but quietly, almost in a whisper.*)

PETER. You still agree, sir, we ought to keep this strictly to ourselves ?
COLONEL. Yes, yes. More anxious to do that than you are. Makes me look a fool—not remembering. But I'm old, y'know, Warton. I was nearly fifty when Diana was born. Too old. I realize that now. Makes a fellow too anxious. Ought to have married much earlier. You married, Warton ?
PETER. No, sir. But I agree that it's about time I was.
COLONEL. Quite so. Marry as soon as you can—and start a family. Don't make my mistake.
PETER. I'll try not to. But never mind about us—let's concentrate on Diana, because I believe if we keep at it, just the two of us, you'll begin to remember, sir.
COLONEL. I'll try, my boy. Very good of you to take the trouble.
PETER (*almost as if doing a lesson*). Diana got married. You remember that now, don't you ?
COLONEL. Yes, yes. Can't think how I came to forget.
PETER (*in the same manner as before*). You weren't very pleased about it.
COLONEL. No, I wasn't.
PETER. Why weren't you ?
COLONEL (*groping ; slowly*). Wasn't what I wanted. Nothing to do with money—that didn't come into it—wrong man—wrong man.
PETER (*distinctly but quietly*). His name was Douglas Barrow.

COLONEL. Yes, of course. Barrow. Stupid of me. Farms a lot of land between Longbridge and Dillingley. Never cared for him. Surly chap—drinks too much. I warned her she was making a fool of herself.

PETER. It didn't last, did it?

COLONEL (*almost automatically*). No, of course not. Told her it wouldn't. She left him—and quite right, too. Surly brute—though quite good family.

PETER (*after a pause ; moving a little nearer to the* COLONEL). Why did she marry him?

COLONEL (*sharply*). That's her business, Warton.

PETER. Right. (*He turns, moves to the fireplace, takes his cigarette case and lighter from his pocket and lights a cigarette.*)

COLONEL (*mildly*). No, my boy. Don't take offence.

PETER (*turning*). I'm not.

COLONEL. Know you mean well.

PETER (*sincerely*). I'm trying to help you, Colonel Risborough.

COLONEL (*struggling to remember*). Yes, yes. Well—of course—I asked her that myself—and—well, you know what the child's like—impulsive—headstrong. (*He pauses.*) There was some fellow before that—one of your Air Force fellows. (*He looks sharply at* PETER.) Wasn't you, was it?

PETER (*quietly but decisively*). No, it wasn't me.

COLONEL. The poor girl had a disappointment—then this chap Barrow kept pressing her—she wanted some sort of security, you know. (*He pauses.*) Never seen or spoken to the chap since she left him—ought to have had a horsewhipping. (*He pauses.*) There was something said about money, too—disgraceful. (*He pauses, then confesses defeat rather brokenly.*) Can't remember for the moment—ought to be ashamed of myself.

PETER. No, you're doing fine, sir. We've only to keep it up—just the two of us—and . . .

(*He breaks off as* MRS PROBUS *enters up* R. *to collect the coffee tray. There is a pause as she moves to* R. *of the coffee table.*)

MRS PROBUS (*surveying the coffee cups*). Somebody hasn't had their coffee.

COLONEL. Miss Lesley. She went out on some errand or other, straight after dinner.

MRS PROBUS. Well, it's all cold now—and I might as well clear. (*She begins to stack the cups and saucers with deliberate slowness.*)

(*The* MAJOR *enters up* R.)

MAJOR (*moving* C. ; *heartily*). Philip, old man, it's a good three-quarters of an hour past your usual time.

COLONEL (*rising ; meekly*). Yes, George. Warton and I were talking . . .

MAJOR. Quite. But he'll have to excuse us now. Old dodderers, y'know, Warton. But I don't suppose Lesley'll be long, and if you've any sense you'll gladly exchange our company for hers.

PETER. Any time. And don't bother about me anyhow, I can amuse myself.

COLONEL (*holding out his hand*). Good night, then, my boy. And —very glad to have you here.

PETER (*shaking hands with the* COLONEL). Good night, sir. Very glad to be here.

(*The* COLONEL *moves up* L.)

MAJOR (*moving up* L.). Help yourself to a drink. 'Night, Warton.

PETER. Thanks. Good night, Major.

(*The* MAJOR *and the* COLONEL *exit up* L. MRS PROBUS, *who has deliberately lingered, looks enquiringly at* PETER, *who looks enquiringly at her.*)

MRS PROBUS (*hesitantly*). Can I tell you something, Mr Warton?

PETER. I wish you would, Mrs Probus.

MRS PROBUS. When you came here yesterday an' the Colonel asked you to stay, I wasn't too pleased. It wasn't just having another one to look after—though there's only me an' a daily woman from the village, though Miss Lesley helps of course, an' there's Huskins for odd jobs. But it wasn't that. It was having somebody coming an' asking questions an' stirring it all up again—you understand, Mr Warton?

PETER. Yes. Very natural.

MRS PROBUS. But I must tell you this—that now you are here, I'm glad you came—'cos I think you've done the Colonel a lot of good already—just having some little talks an' being patient with him—poor old gentleman. I feel a bit better myself, though I couldn't tell you why.

PETER. That's the stuff. And delighted to hear it. Now— would you mind telling *me* something?

MRS PROBUS. I will if I can.

PETER. Oh—this is simple enough. When did Major Buttershaw come here?

MRS PROBUS. Well, he'd often been here—on an' off like—him an' the Colonel being old friends but he didn't come here for good till just after Miss Diana got married. The Colonel felt lonely then —so he asked the Major to come an' stay as long as he liked. So he did. Couldn't do without him now, of course you can see how it is here.

PETER. Yes. Makes himself very useful, doesn't he, the Major?

MRS PROBUS (*confidentially*). That's right—and—if you ask me— takes a bit too much on himself sometimes—though I suppose with the Colonel in the state he's in these days, it's only to be expected. Never been properly himself, the Colonel hasn't, not since Miss Diana was—was taken away from us.

PETER. It's been suggested she deliberately—killed herself.
MRS PROBUS (*vehemently, though in a low tone*). Never never! Don't you believe that tale of her. Nobody knew her better than I did—an' she wasn't that suicide sort at all. Might get into trouble easily enough—might talk a bit wild an' go on about herself—she was always an excitable young madam—but go an' put an end to herself—never never. An' I'll take my dying oath on that.
PETER. An accident then, eh?
MRS PROBUS. Couldn't have been anything else, sir. An' I'll never stop blamin' myself 'cos I didn't go into her bedroom that night. (*She lowers her voice. Confidentially.*) You see, Mr Warton —I couldn't get off to sleep that night—which is unusual for me—but something must have told me—anyhow I couldn't get off an' felt restless—an' then I thought I heard somebody moving about on the main landing—an' I listened, but then I didn't hear any more. But I went down to that landing—where you are, you know—and I listened at her door, but there wasn't a sound and I didn't like to peep in 'cos of disturbing her.
PETER. And you didn't hear anything?
MRS PROBUS. Only the Colonel.
PETER. What was he doing?
MRS PROBUS. He was asleep but making a heavy strangled sort o' breathing noise not like ordinary snoring—but of course that's what it was really. I could hear it right through his thick door.
PETER. And that's all you heard, eh?
MRS PROBUS. That's all.
PETER. And what time was this?
MRS PROBUS. Just after twelve. I remember hearing it strike just when I decided to get up. And when I think that if only I'd gone into Miss Diana, perhaps I might have saved her—then I'll never forgive myself never.
PETER. I wouldn't worry about that, Mrs Probus. You couldn't help it. Just bad luck, that's all.
MRS PROBUS (*picking up the loaded tray*). We're rotten with it here now.
PETER. Bad luck?
MRS PROBUS. Yes, if you want to call it that.
PETER. What do you want to call it?
MRS PROBUS. I haven't a name for it. Kind o' punishment, it sometimes seems to me.

(LESLEY *enters up* R., *leaving the door open. She still has her walking clothes on.*)

PETER. Hello! Any luck?

(MRS PROBUS *moves up* R.)

LESLEY. I'm not sure. Any coffee left?

ACT II]   BRIGHT SHADOW   27

MRS PROBUS. It'll be cold now.
LESLEY. Doesn't matter, then. What about washing up?
MRS PROBUS (*moving to the door up* R.). Finished—except for this lot.

(*She exits up* R. LESLEY *closes the door and moves* C.)

LESLEY. I said I wasn't sure about the luck—because I didn't actually see Douglas Barrow. But I did finally track him down to the *White Hart*, where he's playing in a snooker match, and I left a message asking him to call here when he'd finished. I told him uncle Philip wouldn't be in on it, of course.
PETER. Think he'll come?
LESLEY. I don't know. And I don't really care, either. I only asked him because you insisted on it. Any news from Pam Fotheringham and Ivor Kemp?
PETER. No. But the Colonel's only just gone to bed. He and I were left alone for half an hour—and so we had some more talk.
LESLEY. What about?
PETER. Oh—just this and that.
LESLEY. I think you're a maddening person.
PETER. Not really.
LESLEY. Do you think you'd have got on with Diana?
PETER. I've no idea.
LESLIE. You wouldn't, y'know. I've been thinking about that.
PETER. All right, then. I wouldn't.

(*There is a short pause as* LESLEY *eyes him.*)

LESLEY. Has anybody ever hit you?
PETER. Certainly. Various chaps from time to time.
LESLEY. No girls?
PETER. Not so far. Why?
LESLEY (*wistfully*). Sometimes I'd like to hit you—hard.
PETER. Is that a compliment or not?
LESLEY (*hotly*). No, it isn't. It's just that you seem to me so maddening. And—look here—what are we going to do if all these people turn up together?
PETER (*grinning*). Hold the ring.
LESLEY. It's all right grinning—but it mightn't be so funny. I'm going upstairs to see that both doors along the landing are closed. (*She moves up* L.) And we must see that none of 'em makes a noise in the hall.

(*She exits hastily up* L. *Left to himself,* PETER *looks serious and preoccupied, and after a moment's reflection takes a note-book and pencil from his pocket and makes a note or two. He stares reflectively at what he has written and whistles softly. Suddenly, he looks up and glances at the door up* R. *He replaces the note-book and pencil in his pocket, moves quickly to the door up* R. *and exits, leaving the door open. A murmur of voices is heard off* R., *then he re-enters, ushering in* PAMELA *and* IVOR KEMP. *They both wear outdoor clothes which they do not remove.* IVOR *is about thirty-five, slender, rather good-looking, and precious without being definitely pansy.* PETER *closes the door.* PAMELA *moves* R. *of the settee,* IVOR *stands down* R. *of the easy chair* C.)

PAMELA (*introducing*). This is Ivor Kemp—Peter Warton.
PETER (*moving to* R. *of* IVOR ; *heartily*). How d'you do.
IVOR (*sulkily*). How d'you do.
PAMELA (*to* PETER). And we don't think this is a very good idea.
IVOR. It's a loathsome idea.
PAMELA. Ivor took a great deal of persuading. But he's my guest—and I insisted—so like the nice polite man he is, he had to give in and come along.
PETER. But you don't like the idea either ?
PAMELA. Certainly not.
PETER. Then why did you fall in with it, Mrs Fotheringham ?
PAMELA. Partly because Lesley made such a fuss about it—and partly—curiosity. I can't imagine what you're up to.
IVOR (*still sulkily*). Neither can I.
PAMELA. Not that I'm going to stay while you talk to Ivor. Where *is* Lesley, by the way ?
PETER. She went upstairs to shut some doors—and to try to seal off the older generation.
PAMELA. Well, that's sensible, anyhow. But she might lock a few doors while she's at it. That would make Ivor feel happier, wouldn't it, Ivor ?
IVOR. I'd be happier still if I were away from here. (*Rather defiantly. To* PETER.) And I warn you—I don't intend to stay long.
PETER. I shan't kidnap you.

(LESLEY *enters up* L. *and pauses a moment on the stairs.*)

Can you lock that door ?
LESLEY. Yes.

(*She turns and exits and is heard to lock the door at the head of the stairs. Then she re-enters.*)

PAMELA. Lesley, this is Ivor Kemp. I don't think you've met before, have you ?
LESLEY (*moving below the settee*). No. (*To* IVOR.) How d'you do.
IVOR. How d'you do.
PAMELA (*to* LESLEY). Well, I've brought him—but I'm not staying. I have to run over to the Battersons anyhow—and I wondered if you'd like to come with me, then we can leave these men to themselves.

(LESLEY *flashes an enquiring glance at* PETER, *who nods approval.*)
LESLEY. All right.
IVOR. Don't be long, Pam.
PAMELA (*moving to the door up* R.). Not more than half an hour, I promise. (*To* LESLEY.) Come along, my dear—we'll leave them to it.

(LESLEY *crosses to the door up* R. *and exits with* PAMELA.)

PETER (*turning to* IVOR). You might feel more at home if you took that coat off.
IVOR (*shrugging his shoulders*). I'm not going to feel at home here, whatever I take off. Still . . . (*He removes his overcoat and puts it over the back of the desk chair.*)
PETER. What about a drink?
IVOR. I wouldn't mind some brandy.

(PETER *moves to the sideboard, pours out a brandy, and has the drink ready by the time* IVOR *has removed his overcoat.*)

PETER (*handing the drink to* IVOR). Here you are. And why not sit down?

(IVOR *sits in the easy chair* R.C., *sips his drink, then stares at* PETER, *who eases* L.C.)

IVOR. I don't see how you come into this. And neither does Pam—Mrs Fotheringham.
PETER. I used to be in the Air Force—Bomber Command. There was a girl here who was very nice to us. Beautiful girl. Lively. Wizard type, we thought. Then, after we left, she seems to have gone and made a mess of everything—and died in the rottenest sort of way. Every time I ask about her, somebody tells me something different. Doesn't seem to make sense. I like things to make sense. Worries me when they don't. That's all.
IVOR. Well, I must say it sounds very fishy to me.
PETER. All right, then. It's fishy.
IVOR (*staring at* PETER ; *suddenly*). Look here—are you the man . . . ?
PETER (*interrupting ; sharply*). What man?
IVOR. Either you know or you don't. And if you don't know, then you can't be the man.
PETER. Sounds logical, anyhow.
IVOR (*with some urgency*). Whoever you are, you must know enough to realize that this was a horribly nasty business—that it's done with now—and that there's absolutely no point in stirring it up—and then dragging me into it again.
PETER. Why not?
IVOR (*still urgently*). Because I had quite enough of it at the time —and all I want to do now is to forget it—and give other people a

chance to forget it. Diana's dead—it's all done with—for God's sake—why not leave it alone ?
PETER (*perching himself on the* R. *arm of the easy chair* C.). I can answer that one. She was supposed to be your mistress. Now either she was or she wasn't. If she was, then you ought to be more anxious than anybody to clear things up, for her sake. If she wasn't, then you ought to be anxious to prove that people were wrong when they thought she was your mistress. Either way, it seems to me you're in it up to the neck.
IVOR. What does it matter now ?
PETER. It matters to some people—and I happen to be one of them. Then there's an old man upstairs—two old men, in fact. And a very decent old girl, once her nanny, who still cries a lot and swears that Diana was an angel.
IVOR (*sulkily*). Well, she wasn't.
PETER. Everybody tells me something different. What's your view—you must have known her very well ?
IVOR (*after a pause*). I had a great admiration for Diana. She was lovely to look at—and that means a great deal to me. She wasn't quite as intelligent as lots of people thought—but she had wonderful vitality—could be very charming—and generous, too.
PETER (*coolly*). And—really—as good a mistress as you've ever had.
IVOR (*angrily*). I didn't say that.
PETER. No. As a matter of fact, you haven't said anything yet, have you ?
IVOR. Well, perhaps I'm not going to say anything.
PETER (*softly, but with meaning*). Oh, yes—you are.
IVOR (*with rather feminine defiance*). You can't make me.
PETER (*coldly*). I can have a dam' good try, Kemp.
IVOR (*protesting ; with agitation*). Why are you talking to me like this ? I've done nothing to you. And nobody's asked you to come here—from Burma or wherever it is—and start making mischief. We're doing no harm to you. Why don't you leave us alone ?
PETER (*coldly*). I thought I'd explained that already. There was a girl—a beautiful, lively girl—having a lot of fun—and kind . . .
IVOR. Yes, I know all about that. You said that before.
PETER. Well, then, let's say I had a shock when I heard that she was dead—and how she'd died. And that shock's still here somewhere. And because I can still feel it, let's say that I just don't like the way some of you people, who were all mixed up in her life and her death, seem to take it. I'd like to see it all cleared up. Do you read detective stories ?
IVOR. No. I prefer my fiction to be rather more intelligent and sensitive—to be literature.
PETER. Highbrow type, eh ? Well, I've tried some of this new literature of yours, but most of it seems to be filled with people who don't accept any responsibility and run screaming when they remem-

ber any awkward questions. So when I've time to read, I make do with detective stories.

IVOR. Rather crude, aren't they?

PETER. Yes, no doubt. But they do try to make sense out of the problem they offer you—and don't run away from it. Something's settled in the end.

IVOR. But this isn't a detective story, you know.

PETER. No, but perhaps I'm pretending it is. Just to see what happens.

(*The sound is heard of someone tapping on the window* R.)

IVOR (*rising and turning; startled*). What's that?

PETER (*rising*). Sounds like a visitor.

IVOR (*alarmed*). Who is it?

PETER (*moving to the door up* R.). I don't know till I go and see. Hang on.

(*He exits up* R. IVOR, *left alone, is plainly apprehensive. He finishes his drink, moves and puts his glass on the sideboard, then moves restlessly down* L.C. *as* DOUGLAS BARROW *enters up* R. *He is a burly, red-faced, heavy-featured man in his forties. He wears old tweeds. He has obviously had some drinks but is not drunk.* IVOR, *terrified, stares at him in horror. After a moment, blinking in the light,* BARROW *recognizes* IVOR, *and produces a triumphant chuckle.*)

BARROW (*moving* C.). My God! If it isn't Kemp. (*He chuckles.*) Ivor Kemp! The fellow who can't leave the women alone. The young man with all the sex appeal. Why—I've been waiting for this for years.

IVOR (*backing down* L.; *terrified*). Don't touch me, Barrow.

BARROW. Touch you? Touch you? (*With sudden ferocity.*) Why—you knock-kneed little twerp— (*he moves threateningly towards* IVOR) I'm going to give you the biggest dam' hiding you ever had in your life.

IVOR (*gasping*). No!

(PETER *enters up* R.)

BARROW. And I say—yes.

PETER (*coolly*). But I say—no, too.

BARROW (*turning*). Look—what's—your name . . . ?

PETER (*moving down* R.C.). Warton is the name.

BARROW. Well—look—Warton just keep out of this—and don't interfere.

PETER. Sorry, but I must interfere. I don't say that Kemp couldn't do with a clout or two, but that's not why I asked him to come here, so you're going to leave him alone.

BARROW (*moving to* L. *of* PETER). Will you mind your own dam' business?

PETER. This *is* my business. I invited him here. I also invited you here. But to talk. No rough stuff.
BARROW. Think you can stop it?
PETER. Yes. Now pack it up, Barrow. You're ten years older than I am. You're out of condition. And you've just been doing some serious drinking.
BARROW. Don't worry about me, Warton. I've been in a few fights before—in my time.
PETER. So have I. All kinds. Some with rules—and some without rules.

(*They have now, watching each other closely, moved slowly round until* BARROW *is up stage, and* PETER *directly down stage, covering him.* BARROW *suddenly aims a blow at* PETER *but misses him.* PETER *apparently hits* BARROW *low, then as* BARROW *doubles up,* PETER *hooks him hard on the jaw, and* BARROW *reels back,* L. *of the easy chair* C. PETER *follows up with a knock-out blow apparently on the jaw or the solar plexus.* BARROW *is knocked out.* PETER, *breathing hard, but not damaged, rubs his knuckles, takes a cushion from the easy chair* C. *and puts it under the unconscious* BARROW'S *head as he lies on the floor* L. *of the easy chair* C., *with his head up stage.* IVOR *eases down* C. *and looks in wonder from* BARROW *to* PETER.)

IVOR (*tentatively*). He's—all right—isn't he? I mean—he's not . . . ?
PETER (*interrupting cheerfully*). No, he's just out temporarily. He'll be sitting up asking for a drink in about ten minutes or so. I don't really pack such a punch. (*He moves to the sideboard.*) The fact is—I was clutching about thirty bob's worth of change in my right hand. Cheating, really. (*He pours out a drink for himself.*) But then I'm not here in a sporting capacity—and he was going to be a nuisance. You'd better have another brandy, hadn't you, Kemp?
IVOR. All right, thank you.

(PETER *refills* IVOR'S *glass.*)

I don't know what I'd have done if you hadn't come in. The brute!
PETER (*moving to* IVOR *and handing him the drink*). Well, you know what you can do now, don't you? Talk. And there isn't much time, so let's have the truth. (*He gets his own drink.*)
IVOR. About Diana and me? (*He sits on the settee at the* R. *end of it and puts his glass on the coffee table.*)
PETER (*moving down* C.). Yes, of course. Now this is the story I've been told. You and she were lovers. Barrow found out. She ran out on him—taking some money that wasn't even his—and came to you. But you and she quarrelled about something—she left you late at night—drove back here and had an accident with her car—and died here sometime during the following night. Well, let's take it in order. Were you lovers?

Ivor. No.
Peter. That the truth?
Ivor. Yes.
Peter. Why weren't you?
Ivor (*with an uneasy glance towards* Barrow). Because we weren't.
Peter. That's a woman's answer, Kemp. All right. If you won't tell me anything, I'll tell you something. You've never been any woman's lover—and never wanted to be. That's the truth, isn't it? (*He pauses.*)

(Ivor *looks hesitantly at* Peter.)

(*He moves in to* R. *of* Ivor *and stands dominatingly over him.*) Come on now. Out with it.

Ivor (*breaking*). Yes—dam' you—it is.

(Peter *turns and breaks* C.)

(*Defiantly.*) But then I never said I was. She may have pretended I was—I don't know we were always about together—I'd known her for years.

Peter (*turning*). What was she like—really? Let's have your version.

Ivor. She was rather wonderful in a way—very decorative and amusing—but she was artful—and dominating and rather unscrupulous, as most women are, I suppose. I was frightened of her —in a way.

Peter. Why?

(Ivor *looks at him in silence.*)

All right, I can guess. Because she knew about you—despised you for it.

Ivor. Oh—for God's sake—shut up!

Peter. All right, that's done with. (*He finishes his drink.*) But I'll guess again. (*He moves up* C. *and puts his glass on the sideboard.*) She saw a lot of you—gave people the idea that you were having an affair—because she knew you were safe— (*he moves down* R.C.) and she could make you do what she wanted—and needed a cover for something that *was* real.

Ivor (*startled*). How did you know?

Peter. It's the only explanation—unless she merely needed you to make Barrow jealous—and obviously it wasn't that—because she left him. But what happened when she did leave him—and came to your place?

Ivor. I didn't want her to come to my place. In fact I was furious and told her so. But she said she wasn't staying long—only until the next night. And it was the most convenient place, she said. She didn't want to come here, because of her father; and she didn't want to go to somebody like Pam Fotheringham, because she'd talk too much, I suppose, though Pam had actually been with her when she left Barrow's house that night.

PETER. What had Mrs Fotheringham been doing there?

IVOR (*glancing uneasily towards* BARROW). Wait a minute. What about Barrow?

PETER (*looking down at* BARROW). He's still out. Go on about Mrs Fotheringham. I thought she came into it somewhere.

IVOR. When Diana and Barrow had the big row—which I think she deliberately worked up because she already knew she was going off with this other chap—Barrow went storming out of the house, so Diana rang up Pam and asked her to go over. And when Pam went, Diana told her she was clearing out—and Pam helped her to pack some things. (*He rises and moves to the fireplace.*) Then Diana came over in her car to my place—insisted on staying, although I was furious—made me go up to bed—and stayed downstairs doing some mysterious telephoning.

PETER (*easing down* L.C.). And you had no quarrel the next night, when she left you?

IVOR. No, of course not, though we weren't really friendly because I was still cross about her coming to my place. She left to catch the late train—ten forty-two I think it was—from Longbridge Junction. She admitted that, though she made me promise I wouldn't tell anybody. But though she didn't actually say so, I *knew*—and she knew I knew—that she was going to meet some man at the station and go off with him on that train. And of course that man really was her lover, though where and how she met him—and who he was —I'd no idea.

PETER. But you must have made some guesses about him—eh?

IVOR. She never talked about him—but from one or two remarks she let drop—I guessed that she was terrified about getting him involved in any scandal—and that was one reason why Barrow had to suspect it was me.

PETER. There was no doubt she was really in love with this other man?

IVOR. No, that was obvious. And she was ready to go to any lengths to protect him—including throwing me headfirst into the mess.

PETER (*turning and moving* R.; *musingly*). But why didn't she catch the train?

IVOR. I don't know. She left in good time to catch it. But I never saw her again. All I know is that later that night she drove back here—had an accident—and died sometime the following night. Perhaps the man never turned up at Longbridge Junction—or perhaps there was some change of plan. I don't know. I was sorry for her, of course, but, say what you like, she treated me very badly. You saw what Barrow was like—and some other people weren't too pleasant—and so as soon as the war was over I went back to town. And I hoped that was the last I'd ever hear of the wretched business.

(BARROW *makes a groaning sound and stirs a little.* PETER *moves to* R. *of him.* IVOR *looks alarmed.*)

PETER (*looking down at* BARROW). All right, Barrow, old boy. Don't worry. You're quite happy.

(BARROW *gives a grunt and then settles again.*)

IVOR (*alarmed*). Look here, I'm going to wait outside for Pam.

PETER. He'll be a good five minutes yet before he sits up and takes notice. Just one more thing. I suppose you don't want to do anything for Diana?

IVOR. No. I did enough. She just made use of me—and didn't care what happened to me.

PETER. All right. But I've settled Barrow for you—and it's my belief you'll never need to worry about him again. So will you do something for me?

IVOR. I might. What is it?

PETER. How far is it from your house—I mean, the house you used to have here—and that station—Longbridge Junction?

IVOR. About eleven miles. Why?

PETER. How many garages are there on those eleven miles?

IVOR. Oh, Lord! I can't remember. You go through three villages—probably four or five garages.

PETER. Could you borrow Mrs Fotheringham's car tomorrow?

IVOR. If it was important—yes.

PETER. I think this *is* important—though it's only a hunch. Now do this for me—and for several other people too—Kemp. Borrow her car tomorrow and call at every one of those garages and try to find out for me if Diana didn't call at one of them that night on her way to the station. If anybody looks as if he knows something but won't talk—and he was probably tipped heavily to keep quiet—threaten him with the police.

(LESLEY *enters up* R. *and stands by the door. Owing to the easy chair* C. *being between her and* BARROW, *she does not see him.*)

LESLEY. Pam says she won't come in, but she's ready when you are.

IVOR (*moving above the settee*). I'm just coming. (*He looks at* PETER.) Suppose I do that—what then?

PETER (*forcefully*). Persuade Mrs Fotheringham to bring you over here tomorrow night. Make it a bit later than tonight, if you like. But I'd like to see her as well as you.

IVOR (*dubiously*). Well—I don't know, Warton . . .

PETER. Don't forget Barrow. He knows you're here again. And either we settle all this—or you're in it again up to the neck.

IVOR (*moving* R.). Oh—all right. (*He picks up his overcoat.*) What can I tell Pam? (*He moves to the door up* R.)

PETER. Anything you like. But I want you both here tomorrow night.

(IVOR *and* LESLEY *exit up* R. PETER *moves to the sideboard, damps his handkerchief from the water-jug, then kneels* L. *of* BARROW *and dabs his face.* BARROW *gives a loud grunt or two and begins to recover.* LESLEY *enters up* R. *and moves below the easy chair* C.)

LESLEY (*seeing* BARROW ; *shocked*). Oh—what happened ? Who is it ?

PETER (*softly*). Douglas Barrow. He was going to set about Kemp, so we had a fight and I knocked him out. He's all right.

LESLEY. I must say you seem a brutal bossy type when you get going, Mr Warton.

PETER. I'm not really. Mild as milk as a rule—but this Diana Risborough affair seems to have got me all keyed up.

LESLEY. Because you're still crazy about her.

PETER (*forcefully*). For the last time—*no*.

LESLEY (*half angrily*). And also for the last time—yes—yes—yes. (*She pauses.*) What are we going to do with this poor man ?

PETER. Give him a drink—and ask him some questions. (*To* BARROW.) All right, Barrow. How d'you feel now ? (*He raises* BARROW'S *head and shoulders.*) Like to sit up ?

BARROW (*confusedly*). Who the hell are you ? What happened ? Where's this place ? What's the idea ?

PETER. We had a scrap—and I knocked you out. Just a lucky punch. You're all right. Like to get up ?

BARROW (*struggling to rise*). I *am* getting up. I remember now —young Kemp was here . . . (*He gets to his feet.*)

PETER (*assisting* BARROW *to sit in the easy chair* C.). He's gone now. All over. And no ill feelings, I hope. This is Miss Lesley Dereham—who left the message for you at the pub.

LESLEY (R. *of the easy chair* C.). Hello, Mr Barrow. (*She picks up the cushion and places it behind* BARROW'S *head.*)

BARROW (*groaning*). How d'you do. Leave a message for a fella —an' then knock him for six. Dam' silly idea. Got a drink ?

PETER (*moving to the sideboard*). Certainly. Whisky ?

BARROW. Thanks. And not too much soda.

(PETER *pours out a whisky and soda for* BARROW.)

(*He rubs his jaw and generally pulls himself together.*) How's the Colonel these days ? I've only just got back.

LESLEY. He's not very well. He—never really recovered—from —from the shock, you know.

BARROW. Sorry to hear it—though he never liked me. But perhaps he isn't the only one who never really recovered.

(PETER *moves to* L. *of* BARROW *and hands him the whisky and soda.*)

(*He takes the glass.*) Thanks. Need this. Well—cheers ! (*He takes a long drink.*) That's better. Anybody got a cigarette ? I'm out of 'em.

(LESLEY *gets the box of cigarettes and matches from the sideboard and offers them to* BARROW, *who takes a cigarette and lights it during the following speeches.* LESLEY *then returns the cigarette box and matches to the sideboard and perches herself on the* L. *arm of the easy chair* R.C.)

PETER (*easing below the coffee table*). I'm sorry about the scrap, Barrow.

BARROW. I'm not complaining, what's—your—name Warton, isn't it ? I'm older than you—but let me have a week's training and you wouldn't land one as easily as that.

PETER. Probably not. But I had to interfere between you and Kemp because I wanted to talk to him, just as I want to talk to you. Same subject—Diana.

BARROW. You're out of luck, Warton. The subject's closed—for good. And if you'll just allow me to finish this drink and cigarette, then I'll make tracks.

(PETER *and* LESLEY *exchange looks.*)

LESLEY. You don't mind if we talk, Mr Barrow ?

BARROW. I can't stop you. So go ahead.

LESLEY (*to* PETER). Did you get anything from Ivor Kemp ?

PETER. Lots. I guessed at once he wasn't the type of bloke a girl like Diana would fall in love with and run away to join. And she knew his little secret. He looks like a bit of camouflage—and that's what she used him for—just camouflage, to hide a really serious situation that was developing with somebody else—a real man.

BARROW. Now—wait a minute . . .

PETER (*ignoring the interruption*). When she joined him that night, she merely went to hide away for twenty-four hours until she could join this other man on the late train from Longbridge Junction. There was no question of a quarrel with Kemp, except that he was annoyed at her being there at all.

LESLEY. Why didn't she catch that train, then ? Didn't the man turn up ? Or did she miss it—or what ?

PETER. That's something we don't know—yet.

LESLEY (*staring at* PETER ; *meaningly*). *Are you sure you don't know ?*

PETER (*looking steadily at* LESLEY *and imitating her tone*). *Yes, Lesley, I'm sure I don't know.*

LESLEY (*coldly*). I didn't know I'd asked you to call me Lesley.

(BARROW, *who has been deeply attentive, is unable to contain himself any longer.*)

BARROW. Never mind whether you asked him to call you Lesley or not—this is serious.

LESLEY. So is that—to me.

BARROW (*ignoring* LESLEY ; *to* PETER). Is that the truth, Warton —the honest truth ?

PETER. I believe it is. Besides, you ought to have guessed long ago. Look at Kemp!

BARROW. That's what made it so much worse. First, to be deceiving an' making a fool of me—then to run off, and take money with her that didn't belong to me—all for a knock-kneed squeaking little twerp like Kemp.

PETER. You can make your mind up, Barrow—that whoever it was, it was somebody very different from Kemp.

BARROW. Well, that's something. If I'd only known at the time —though even then, of course, it would have been hard to take. (*He finishes his drink, then looks at his glass.*) If we're going to talk, I'd better have another of those.

LESLEY (*rising and taking the glass from* BARROW). Don't move. I'll do it. Big one?

BARROW. Enormous.

(LESLEY *moves to the sideboard and pours out a large whisky and soda for* BARROW.)

(*He looks at* PETER.) What are you up to in all this?

PETER (*sitting on the settee*). Just shaking the bag a bit, and then seeing what comes out. It's having results already.

BARROW. So it seems, though I don't quite see the point. But if that's true about Kemp—and I can see now it might be—I'm ready to talk if you want me to.

(LESLEY *moves to* R. *of* BARROW *and hands him the drink.*)

(*He takes the drink.*) Thanks. That's what I call a whisky and soda. Cheers! (*He takes a long drink.*)

LESLEY (*sitting in the easy chair* R.C.). Were you very much in love with Di?

BARROW (*gruffly*). Yes. Had been for years before I married her. Still am, in a way, though I've called her a lot of names I wouldn't like to repeat to you. And she deserved 'em, too. She never tried to make a proper go of our marriage, though I did everything I could to please her, including getting myself in debt. She wouldn't settle down properly and give me a hand. She went on chucking money away when I warned her we couldn't afford it. She went off the deep end every time I tried to reason with her. She lied to me. She cheated. She stole. She gave me a hell of a time. But it didn't make any difference. She was the one I wanted, and the only one I'll ever want. And I'd willingly go through it all again—just for the sake of the few times when she remembered to be decent to me. I know I'm supposed to be a surly devil—but I wasn't with her. These stories that I treated her badly aren't true—except right at the end when I knew I'd lost her—but up to then I was always too far gone—barmy about her. Still am, really—and sometimes late at night it starts all over again—until I could knock my dam' thick head against the wall.

LESLEY. Why did you two marry? I've always wondered.

BARROW. I married her because I wanted her—had done for years and years—ever since she was a kid. She married me because some other fellow disappointed her—so she took me just to spite him. That's why it didn't work, of course. Very soon everything I said or did seemed too dull for her. You know what I mean. I'd try an' try—but everything'd be dull—and by gad—soon I began to feel myself it was dull—and that was torture—see what I'm getting at?

LESLEY (*warmly*). I do. I know exactly. And I'm sorry. You're quite different from what I expected.

BARROW. Thanks—I'll take that as a compliment. But you can see what happened. Di was always extravagant but it didn't matter before she married, because the old Colonel's very well off and doted on her. But I had to be careful—and I warned her about that from the start. Then, of course, her pals went about saying I was mean an' cruel to her, when in fact I'd run myself into debt and the whole farm into danger trying to please her. That's why that money thing hit me hardest of all because she must have known dam' well that money wasn't mine.

PETER. Tell us about that money, Barrow.

BARROW. I was secretary and treasurer of the local Stockbreeders' Association in those days. This money belonged to the Association —nearly three hundred pounds—some fivers and tenners, but mostly in pound and ten bob notes—so it was quite a packet. I'd left it lying on my desk because I was going to check it that night before paying it into the bank next morning. But we had this big row about Kemp—and I barged out of the house to see if a walk down to the pub would do me any good. When I came back, she'd gone—and the money had gone with her. The next time I hear anything—two days later—she's dead. I had to make that money good, of course —and had to sell some dam' fine beasts to do it. After that I cleared out—got a temporary job with a cousin of mine in Kenya.

PETER. Nothing was said at the inquest about this money, was it?

BARROW. Hell—no! Why give 'em more muck to dish up? But it hurt me like the devil. Still does.

LESLEY. Yes, of course. (*Wonderingly.*) But that doesn't sound like Diana, you know.

BARROW. I'd have said that—but—once a woman marries the wrong bloke she doesn't seem to care what she does. Well . . . (*He finishes his drink, rises, and puts his glass on the coffee table.*)

PETER (*rising*). Just one more question. What became of that money?

BARROW (*staring at* PETER; *surprised*). How should I know? She'd taken it—that was enough. I thought she'd probably given it to her fancy boy—Kemp.

PETER. But, you see, Kemp didn't mean anything to her. She

was going away with somebody else. And if she had that money she'd have taken it with her to the station. We don't know if she ever got to the station—or what happened—but we do know that later that night she had an accident on her way here—and was brought back here and put to bed. Well, then, what became of the money? As you say, it must have made quite a packet—not like new notes straight from the bank. You'd think somebody would have noticed a parcel of money that size.

BARROW (*shrugging his shoulders*). Never thought of that. Didn't know Kemp wasn't the boy friend, of course—and I'm dam' glad to know he wasn't. Grateful for that, Warton. But still, she took the money—and I can't get over that. Hurts, y'know—that—an' waking up at night—wanting her back, whatever she did—an' wondering how an' why life turns into such a damnably nasty mess. (*He moves to the door up* R.) Must push off. 'Night, Miss Dereham.

(LESLEY *rises*.)

PETER (*moving to the door up* R.). I'll see you out, Barrow. Sorry about the scrap we had—but glad you came.

(BARROW *and* PETER *exit up* R. LESLEY *looks thoughtful, moves up* L., *and exits. She is heard to unlock the door at the head of the stairs. Then she re-enters, moves to the settee and sits uncomfortably on it, looking a forlorn figure. After a moment or two*, PETER *re-enters up* R., *closes the door and moves to* R. *of the settee*. LESLEY *ignores him, and he looks at her for a moment, speculatively*.)

(*Quietly*.) What's the matter?
LESLEY. I'm feeling miserable.
PETER. I thought you were. Why?
LESLEY (*evasively*). Perhaps I'm tired. I'll go to bed in a minute.
PETER. All right—we'll leave it at that. (*He sits in the easy chair* C.)
LESLEY (*with more energy*). No—we won't. I suppose I'm feeling miserable because all this wretched business about poor Diana seems more and more confusing—and—and unsatisfactory—and depressing. It wasn't so bad when I thought it was all Douglas Barrow's fault—or mostly his fault—and I could dislike him because he was so mean and cruel—and treated her so badly. But it seems it wasn't like that—and I feel sorry for him, even if he *is* so stupid. And I feel sorry for poor Ivor Kemp, too—instead of being angry with him. And that makes it all the more complicated—and unsatisfactory—and depressing. I feel now everything was Diana's fault—she comes out of it much worse than she did—but—look what happened to her—so I can't blame her really—and still feel sorry for her, too.
PETER (*after a short pause*). Every time anybody talks about her, I

get an entirely different picture. Now she's this—now she's that. Well, I suppose that could mean various things.

LESLEY (*snappishly*). And one of them is—that you can't know much about her yourself.

PETER. But I never said I did.

LESLEY. You came here—talking almost as if you owned her. Or she owned you.

PETER. Then you can't have listened to what I said.

LESLEY (*annoyed*). Oh—don't start on again about a beautiful girl dying—and you out in Burma with all your lovely golden memories—and trying to make sense out of some pieces of life.

PETER (*angrily*). All right I won't, then. Forget it.

LESLEY (*rising*). All I want you to tell me now is just one thing—and then you needn't tell me any more.

PETER (*rising*). What's that?

LESLEY (*deliberately*). Why didn't you meet her that night at the station?

PETER. But...

LESLEY (*sharply*). No, don't start humming and hawing and dodging—and trying to be clever and mysterious. All I want is a plain answer to a plain, sensible question—and then, as far as I'm concerned, the great mystery of my poor cousin Diana is solved.

PETER (*gravely*). You're wrong, you know. It wouldn't be solved.

LESLEY. It would for me.

PETER (*annoyed*). You don't know what you're talking about.

LESLEY. Oh—shut up! You make me so angry.

(*As they stand glaring at each other, the* MAJOR *enters up* L. *He wears bedroom slippers, old trousers, a warm thick dressing-gown and a faded scarf. He smokes a pipe.* PETER *and* LESLEY *turn, startled, and look at him. He regards them quizzically, then moves* C.)

MAJOR. Sorry to disturb you—though you both look extremely annoyed.

LESLEY (*shortly*). We are. (*She breaks to the fireplace.*)

MAJOR. Couldn't sleep and felt restless—so I decided I might as well have a drink with my pipe. (*He moves to the sideboard and pours out a whisky and soda for himself.*) Now—don't start glaring at each other again. Take it easy. And tell me what you've learnt from these various visitors you've had.

PETER (*easing* R.C.). You heard them—then?

MAJOR. Heard 'em coming and going—that's all. The Colonel didn't notice anything. (*He turns and moves to the settee with his drink.*) Who came?

LESLEY. Pamela Fotheringham, Ivor Kemp, Douglas Barrow.

MAJOR (*sitting on the settee*). Well—well well! Find out anything we didn't know?

PETER (*perching himself on the* L. *arm of the easy chair* R.C.). Yes, though it doesn't all make sense yet.
MAJOR. Keeping it to yourself—or would you like to tell me?
PETER. First, I'd rather ask you a question.
MAJOR. Why not? Go ahead, Warton.
PETER. Barrow says Diana took nearly three hundred pounds in used notes from his desk, that night she cleared out. Now that's quite a bulky amount to carry. When she was brought back here after her accident with the car, late the following night, had she still that money with her?
MAJOR. No, she had between twenty and thirty pounds in her handbag—and no money in either of her suitcases.
PETER. What became of that money, then?
MAJOR (*shrugging his shoulders*). No idea—and I can't see it matters much. I assumed she'd given it to Kemp before they quarrelled.
PETER. We know now that Kemp wasn't her lover and never had been, and that there wasn't any quarrel. She left him to catch a train at Longbridge Junction.
MAJOR (*coolly*). She said something about catching a train when we brought her back here.
PETER. Why didn't you say so before?
MAJOR. My dear chap, I didn't pretend to do anything last night but give you a bare summary of the chief facts. We were in a hurry, you remember.
LESLEY. But what could have become of all that money?
MAJOR (*shrugging his shoulders*). Anything. She may have thrown it away.
LESLEY. That's silly.
PETER (*to the* MAJOR). And I don't think you're being much of a help.

(*The* MAJOR *regards them calmly, takes a drink, puts his glass on the coffee table, then re-lights his pipe.*)

MAJOR. I thought last night, Warton, that you were going to ask a few questions and then leave us. Now it looks as if you're seriously trying your hand at some sort of investigation.
PETER. I am.
MAJOR (*mildly*). So I gather. I don't know what your qualifications are . . .
PETER. I haven't any.
MAJOR (*quietly*). Well—I suggest you drop it.
PETER (*quietly*). Can I ask why?
MAJOR (*slowly and quietly*). Because you can't do any good—and you might easily do a lot of harm.
PETER. I don't see that.
MAJOR. You must take my word for it, Warton.
PETER. I'm afraid I can't do that, Major Buttershaw. You see,

already the whole story looks very different from the one you told me yesterday. And I can't stop now.

MAJOR. You're making it very difficult for me.

PETER. Difficult—to do what ?

MAJOR. To keep quiet. Though, if I've any sense, that's what I shall do.

LESLEY (*eagerly*). I always knew there was *something* you were keeping to yourself—always.

MAJOR (*turning to* LESLEY). Lesley, I don't think you ought to hear this. You won't like it.

LESLEY. Probably not. But I refuse to go—if that's what you want.

MAJOR. Well, don't say I didn't warn you. And I shall have to trust you both. I know you're all right, Lesley. But—I've got to take a chance with you, Warton. Unless you promise here and now to drop this investigating of yours.

PETER. I'm sorry, Major, but I can't do that.

MAJOR. Then you force me out into the open. (*He picks up his glass, finishes the drink, then holds the glass out to* LESLEY.) Would you mind, my dear ? I think I shall need another.

(LESLEY *takes the glass, moves to the sideboard and pours out another whisky and soda for the* MAJOR.)

(*He turns to* PETER.) If you've been using your wits these last twenty-four hours, then two things ought to have struck you, my boy. First—the Colonel. He's an old man, it's true—but not in his dotage—yet his only child dies, the daughter he almost worshipped and certainly spoilt—and now he can't remember her death or any of the circumstances that led up to it. Shock ? Defence mechanism ? Yes—but why ? That's the first question you ought to have asked yourself, Warton.

(LESLEY *moves to* R. *of the settee and stands holding the* MAJOR'S *drink.*)

PETER. Perhaps I have. But what's the other thing ?

MAJOR. Diana herself. You talk a lot about making sense out of things, but what sense can you make out of her and her story ? I'll bet everybody you've talked to so far has given you a different account of her, haven't they ?

PETER. Yes. Quite different.

MAJOR. I thought so. Well, look at it. She marries a man she doesn't really want. She pretends to have a lover. She leaves her husband and takes money that completely disappears. She thinks she has to meet somebody at a railway station, yet comes driving here at midnight, hell-for-leather. Don't you see that it doesn't make sense, because there's no sense in it or in her ? And the answer's simple enough, especially if you take into account what her father's like.

LESLEY (*perturbed*). You mean—she wasn't sane ?
MAJOR (*coolly*). Of course.
(PETER *rises and breaks down* R.)
Just as, strictly speaking, her father isn't sane. Don't forget I was his medical officer once. He was always unstable—liable to temporary fits of insanity. We're old friends—but there's this other bond between us—that I know—and he knows I know.
LESLEY. But he's my uncle—Diana was my cousin—surely I'd have known . . .
MAJOR (*gently*). Why should you, my dear ? After all, how much time did you spend with either of them ? I've known them both far better than you've done—medically, too. And I must say something about myself here, to make you understand where I fit into the picture. At the risk of boring you.
PETER (*moving to the easy chair* R.C. ; *rather grimly*). You're not boring me, Major. (*He sits.*)
MAJOR. I've known Philip Risborough over forty years. We served together. I was with him in India and I was M.O. of the battalion he commanded in the First World War. And we're not only old friends—but, what's more important—close friends.
LESLEY. Yes, of course.
MAJOR. After Diana married, the Colonel asked me to come and stay with him here—and stay as long as I liked. Now I'll be frank with you—I needed that invitation badly. I'd come to the end of my last little temporary war job and was living from hand-to-mouth in a little bed-sitting room in a dingy back street—never mind where, but I never want to set eyes on the place again. And I was wondering just how much longer life could be worth living. I'm putting my cards on the table, you see, and in a minute you'll know why. Well, the Colonel pulled me out of that—gave me everything I could reasonably want here. Partly out of old friendship, of course—and for companionship—but also—and this didn't make me feel any the less grateful—because he knew I could keep an eye on him, knowing his history as I did. (*He takes his drink from* LESLEY.) Thank you, my dear.

(LESLEY *sits in the easy chair* C.)

I find telling the truth thirsty work. (*He drinks, places his glass on the coffee table, then looks gravely at them for a moment.*) I found that he was already beginning to be desperately worried about Diana. They'd had some scenes about this marriage of hers. He was worried about himself, too. And I didn't like the look of either of them, knowing what I did. I had some difficult times with him. But he was my friend—I owed him everything I had here—and I couldn't complain, and did what I could. Then Barrow rang up, late one night, cursing and blinding, to tell us she'd left him. The Colonel was almost out of his mind himself, and was convinced she was out of her mind, and though I pretended to disagree with him, I wasn't sure. But I spent most of the next day persuading him not to take any action—God knows what he didn't want to do—and then late that night we had the police message about her accident, and got her back here safe into bed. I gave both of them strong sedatives—and took risks—but none of us wanted a doctor from outside here. We got through the day somehow. Then that night I gave the Colonel another sedative, saw him settled, and then gave Diana, who was complaining and rambling in her speech, about twelve grains of barbiturate. She was quieter but not asleep when I left. I came down here for a drink or two, but kept listening. Then I must have dropped off to sleep in the chair for an hour or so—I was dog-tired and short of sleep—and when I woke, around midnight, I went up the stairs (*he points up* L.) here and could hear both their voices, loud and angry. But before I got up to her room, the voices had stopped. Dead silence. I thought the Colonel must have gone back to his room and went along there—but his bed was empty. I looked into both bathrooms and my own room—like a fool, because every second was precious, and it seemed reasonable to suppose he'd left Diana when it was all so quiet, and, not finding him there, I went along to Diana's room. There was a light on above the bed. He was standing there white and shaking—with a completely blank look on his face. And Diana was dead.

LESLEY (*in horror*). Oh ! (*She quietly begins to break down and starts to sob.*)

MAJOR (*very quietly*). Without knowing what he was doing and of that I'm certain—he'd killed her.

PETER (*very quietly*). How had he killed her ?

MAJOR. He must have smothered her.

(PETER *rises and moves down* R.)

She was shaky after the accident, remember, and half doped with the barbiturate. And in spite of his age, he was strong, especially in one of his insane rages.

PETER (*quietly*). I see. (*He moves* R.C.) So what did you do ?

MAJOR. I tried to resuscitate her first, of course. But that was hopeless. I got the Colonel back into his bed—he was just like a child and had no idea what had happened, hasn't yet, and never will have, in my opinion. Then I went back to Diana's room. I had to make it look like an accident—or, at the worst—suicide. What else could I do ? I had to take a chance—so left the half-empty box of barbiturates by her bedside, arranged the body . . .

LESLEY (*through her sobs ; protestingly*). No—not that.

MAJOR. Sorry, Lesley. But I didn't want you to hear this, you remember. Anyhow, I did what was necessary—to make it look as if she'd died in her sleep during the night—and left it at that. Fortunately my evidence was accepted. I had to bluff it out. Nothing I did could bring the girl back to life, and I didn't see why my old

friend should spend the rest of his life in a criminal lunatic asylum.
LESLEY (*crying*). No, of course not.
MAJOR. You see what he's like now. He doesn't remember—and never will. And he's happy in his own way. I'm here to look after him. And there's been no scandal—no fuss. In fact, the whole miserable business has been almost forgotten—until you turned up yesterday, Warton.
PETER (*softly*). And that's why you're telling me this?
LESLEY (*stormily*). Of course!
MAJOR (*carefully*). I've taken the risk of telling you the truth—though, mind you, I'd deny every word of it and laugh in your face if the police were present—because I wanted you to understand why I advised you to drop this little investigation of yours. Why I told you it can't do any good—and might easily do a lot of harm. (*He picks up his glass, finishes his drink, replaces the glass on the coffee table, rises and looks sympathetically at the softly-weeping* LESLEY.) Now, Lesley!
LESLEY (*checking herself*). It's all right—I'll be better in a minute. (*She pauses.*) Poor Uncle Philip!
MAJOR (*quietly*). That's what I thought. Well— (*he looks at them for a moment*) that's that. (*He moves up* L.) Good night.

(*He exits up* L. *There is a pause.* LESLEY *dabs at her face with her handkerchief.* PETER *is thoughtful.*)

PETER (*tonelessly*). Yes—that's that.
LESLEY (*rising quickly; angrily*). How can you talk like that? I really *do* hate you now.
PETER (*mildly*). But why?
LESLEY. Can't you see what you've done by coming here—and asking questions—interfering? And you don't even *care*.

(PETER *takes a step or two towards* LESLEY.)

Keep away from me. I hope you're leaving in the morning. I wish you'd never come here.
PETER. Sorry you feel like that.
LESLEY. Well, I do. (*She moves up* L.) And I'm going to bed.
PETER. Good idea. But I'm not leaving in the morning, you know.
LESLEY (*stopping and turning*). And why not?
PETER (*softly*). Because I don't believe a word of the Major's story.
LESLEY (*astonished*). But—Peter—it *must* be true.
PETER. Why must it?
LESLEY. Because—because—he couldn't have told us such a horrible story if it hadn't been true.
PETER. And I think he couldn't have told it if it *had* been true. And before I go I'll prove I'm right.

LESLEY. But—but . . .
PETER (*interrupting ; quietly*). You just think it over quietly. I'm going to, Lesley. Good night.

LESLEY *stands staring at him as—*

the CURTAIN *falls quickly.*

ACT III

SCENE.—*The same. Late the following evening.*

When the CURTAIN *rises, coffee is set on the coffee table. The curtains are closed, the fire is burning cheerfully and all the lights are on.* LESLEY *is seated on the settee at the* R. *end of it, busily sewing. The* COLONEL *is seated on the settee,* L. *of her, quietly ruminating. The* MAJOR *is seated in the easy chair* R.C. *He is reading " The Times " and smoking his pipe. The scene at a first glance is a very tranquil domestic one, but after a moment or two we realize that* LESLEY *is rather uneasy and jumpy and that she exchanges some glances with the* COLONEL. *Only the* MAJOR, *sitting very snug, appears to be really at ease.*

COLONEL (*after a long pause*). Well, I must say, I've missed young Warton's company tonight more than I imagined I should. Hoped he'd be back before now to tell us what he's been up to.

(*The* MAJOR *lowers his paper and looks at his watch.*)

MAJOR. Philip, it's an hour past your usual time.

COLONEL (*easily*). I thought it was, George.

MAJOR (*rising*). Won't do, y'know, old man. (*He folds the paper and puts it on the desk.*) Easiest thing in the world, once you start, to break up a sensible routine—and then you're all over the place.

COLONEL. Agree with you in theory, George. But the fact remains—the last day or two I've felt much better.

LESLEY (*looking up from her work*). I've been wondering about that, Uncle Philip. Because I think you've been looking much better.

MAJOR (*easing* C. ; *heartily*). Don't bother about me, you two. I'm only the old medico round here. I wouldn't know what's good for anybody. No—seriously, old man   high time we went up. And no chess tonight, I think   half an hour of Russian Bank perhaps, eh ?

COLONEL (*rising slowly*). All right. And Warton can tell me his adventures—if he's had any—in the morning. (*He moves up* L.)

MAJOR (*moving up* L.). Perhaps they aren't the kind of adventures he'd want to tell anybody. (*He chuckles, then turns and looks at* LESLEY.) And if you take *my* tip, Lesley, *you* won't stay up too late tonight, either. You're looking tired.

LESLEY. I feel a bit washed out. Good night.

COLONEL. Good night, my dear.

ACT III] BRIGHT SHADOW 49

MAJOR. Good night.

(*The* COLONEL *and the* MAJOR *exit up* L. LESLEY *puts her work down on the settee rather impatiently, and gives the impression of being puzzled and rather anxious. She makes small restless movements and taps her fingers on the arm of the settee. After a few moments, she rises, crosses quickly to the window, draws the curtains aside a little and peers out. She then turns impatiently and moves restlessly* R.C. MRS PROBUS *enters up* R.)

MRS PROBUS (*moving to the coffee table*). I've about done now, Miss Lesley. But I'll take these coffee things. (*She stacks the cups and saucers.*)

LESLEY. Yes, do.

MRS PROBUS. Is it worth while keeping anything hot for Mr Warton?

LESLEY. No, I don't think it is. If he hasn't had any dinner—and he's hungry when he comes in—I can find something cold for him. Don't you bother.

MRS PROBUS. Then I'll just take this little lot—an' then finish.

LESLEY (*after a pause*). Mrs Probus.

MRS PROBUS (*looking up*). Yes?

LESLEY. When Diana was brought here after that accident she had with her car, did you unpack her bags?

MRS PROBUS (*surprised*). Yes. Two cases. Why?

LESLEY. Was there a lot of money—about three hundred pounds —in one of them?

MRS PROBUS. No, of course there wasn't. I'd have said if there had been. Is somebody accusing me . . . ?

LESLEY (*interrupting quickly*). No, Mrs Probus, nobody's accusing you. I just wanted to know, that's all.

MRS PROBUS. What for?

LESLEY. She's supposed to have had all this money, and nobody knows what she did with it. Do you think—she could have just thrown it away?

MRS PROBUS (*astonished*). Course she couldn't. I never heard of anything so silly. She might have been a bit extravagant an' careless —poor lamb—as I know better than the next one, looking after her an' her things for years the way I did—but—throwing away hundreds o' pounds—of course not.

LESLEY. Well, it disappeared somehow. And—and if she was temporarily out of her mind . . .

MRS PROBUS (*shocked and astonished*). Out of her mind?

LESLEY (*rather desperately*). Yes—a sudden—sort of fit of insanity . . .

MRS PROBUS (*indignantly*). Now—who's been stuffing you up with these tales? Poor thing was no more out of her mind than you are. She was upset about something—she'd had a nasty little accident and I don't say she mightn't have had one too many of these Martinis or gins-an'-limes or whatever they are—but that's all. I've been nearer bein' out o' my mind than she ever was.

LESLEY (*bewildered*). But—but—as Peter says—it doesn't make sense.

MRS PROBUS (*pointedly*). Oh—it's " as Peter says " now, is it ?

LESLEY (*indignantly*). No, it isn't—so you needn't start any of that. But it's true—as he says—it just doesn't make sense—I mean, what she did—everything that happened.

MRS PROBUS (*darkly*). Ah now you're talking, Miss Lesley. I've always said that—an' I always will. (*She moves to* LESLEY *and lowers her voice. More darkly.*) An' I'll tell you another thing. There's some know a lot more about it than they've ever let on to know. (*She turns to the coffee table and picks up the tray.*)

(*As she does so,* PETER *enters hastily up* R. *He wears his raincoat and carries his hat.*)

PETER. Oh—they're not here yet ?
LESLEY. Who ?
PETER. Kemp and Mrs Fotheringham.
LESLEY. Perhaps they're not coming.
PETER. If they don't turn up in the next quarter of an hour, we'll ring her up.

(*He turns and exits up* R. *to put away his hat and raincoat.* MRS PROBUS *moves* C. *with the tray.*)

MRS PROBUS (*to* LESLEY ; *in a low voice*). Sweet on him, aren't you ?

LESLEY (*snappishly*). Certainly not !

MRS PROBUS (*moving to the door up* R. ; *chuckling*). Then you ought to be.

(PETER *enters up* R. *and holds the door open for* MRS PROBUS, *who nods meaningly at him as she exits.* PETER *grins, then closes the door behind her.*)

LESLEY (*moving to the fireplace*). I've just been talking to Mrs Probus. She knew a lot about Diana, you know—adored her.

PETER (*moving down* C.). I know she did. Biased, no doubt—but nevertheless a very useful witness.

LESLEY. I wish you wouldn't talk like a detective.

PETER. Sorry, but it's because I feel I ought to think and act like one now. And what did Mrs Probus say ?

LESLEY. She said she unpacked Diana's two cases that night after the accident, and that there wasn't any money in them. Then when I suggested that Di might have thrown the money away because she really wasn't right in her head just then, Mrs Probus said that was absolute nonsense—and that there was nothing really wrong with Di. And now I simply can't make head or tail of it all. Where have you been ?

PETER. Longbridge Junction. And I had to wait until a character called Old Judd came on duty there. How was the Colonel tonight?
LESLEY. Better. He admitted he was, and I said he looked better, too. What were you talking to him about all the afternoon?
PETER. Oh—this and that.
LESLEY (*annoyed*). Don't be so maddening. Why don't you tell me something?
PETER. Because I'm not sure. It's still tricky. And there isn't time to start because Kemp and Mrs Fotheringham may be here any minute. And—listen—you told me Mrs Fotheringham was uneasy and had something to hide. Are you sure?
LESLEY. I'm sure she was uneasy, two days ago, when you first came, but I can't be certain she's hiding something. I just feel she is, that's all. But what it can be, I can't imagine.
PETER. Will you do something for me?
LESLEY. Perhaps.
PETER. When Kemp and Mrs Fotheringham arrive, I don't want you to be here. I shall deal with him first—he's all right and won't be any trouble—and as soon as I've done with him I shall ask him to go out to the car and wait. Then I'll take on Mrs Fotheringham, who's a much tougher nut to crack. And that's where I want your help.
LESLEY (*sarcastically*). I didn't know you ever needed anybody's help.
PETER. No cracks—there isn't time.
LESLEY. Well, what do I do?
PETER. The trouble is—I don't know. But if you can think of anything that might frighten the Fotheringham woman—give her a shock—and so help me to break her down, I want you to try it. If you keep an eye on the front door from upstairs, you'll know when Kemp has gone—and it's then I want some assistance from you to deal with the beautiful Pamela.
LESLEY. You don't think she's beautiful, do you?
PETER. I can't stand the woman.
LESLEY. Neither can I. I'd enjoy frightening her out of her skin. But how to do it is another thing. And you be careful—she's a man-eater. I only wish . . .

(PETER *suddenly holds up his hand, checks her and glances towards the door up* R.)

PETER (*softly*). They're here. Pop off, Lesley. Try to think of something—while I create a sinister atmosphere.

(LESLEY *exits quickly up* L. PETER *turns and exits up* R. *He re-enters almost immediately, ushering in* IVOR *and* PAMELA. *Both wear overcoats but no hats.* PAMELA *carries her handbag.*)

PAMELA (*as she enters*). So really I'm here to see that you don't bully poor Ivor. (*She moves* C.) And I warn you, we're not staying

long. (*She glances around the room.*) Hate this dam' room—always have. Must be dreadful staying here, isn't it ?
PETER (*moving to the fireplace*). I've enjoyed myself so far. (*He stands with his back to the fireplace.*) But I shan't be here much longer. Might possibly be able to leave tomorrow.
PAMELA (*sitting on the settee*). You talk as if you'd come here to do a job.
PETER (*grimly*). I have, Mrs Fotheringham. Sit down, Kemp.

(IVOR *moves to the easy chair* R.C. *and sits.*)

I've been very busy, too. Only came in a few minutes ago—and so had to miss dinner.
IVOR. You don't think you're wasting your time ?
PETER. No, I know I'm not. Well, did you try those garages ?
IVOR. Yes—and you were right. I found the one she called at, about four miles from the station. The man didn't want to say anything—she'd asked him not to and given him a good tip—but I persuaded him—had to give him something—too.
PETER. How much ?
IVOR. Thirty bob—all I had with me.

(PETER *takes his wallet from his pocket, and extracts three ten-shilling notes.*)

PETER. The firm pays. (*He crosses to* IVOR.) Thirty bob. (*He hands the notes to* IVOR.)
IVOR (*taking the notes and putting them in his pocket*). Thanks.

(PETER *perches himself on the* R. *arm of the chair* C.)

The garage was closed, of course, but this chap lives next door and keeps his ears open. She came running up, breathless, and told him the car was about a quarter of a mile along the road, that she couldn't get it to go, and she was in a hurry. He went back with her—it was a stoppage in the feed pipe—and it didn't take him long—but of course she'd wasted a lot of time trying to restart the car and fetching him—and he said it was well after half past ten when the car was going again. And that would explain why—if she was trying to catch the ten forty-two at Longbridge Junction—she missed it.
PETER. She did miss it. I've just been to Longbridge Junction and I've spoken to the porter—one Judd—who remembers her missing it. He remembers her because when he told her it had gone—and a certain gentleman had gone with it—first, she took out a flask of brandy and had a pull at it ; then she gave him a taste ; and then she burst into tears. And as old porters don't have adventures like that every night with strange beautiful young ladies, he remembers it very well. There's no doubt it was Diana.
PAMELA. So that's it. I've wondered—and wondered.
PETER. You knew she had planned to run away with some man ?

PAMELA. I guessed it more or less—though I didn't know how—when—where—or who he was. I gathered it was important that nobody had to know who he was.

PETER (*rising*). Well, this part of the story is now fairly clear. She arranged with some man to catch the ten forty-two that night at Longbridge Junction. He caught it and went off, probably thinking she'd decided not to join him. She missed it—didn't want to go back to Kemp's place—so decided to come here.

IVOR (*rising*). I don't think there's anything else I can tell you, Warton.

PAMELA (*rising*). And so we can go now.

PETER. I can't stop you.

PAMELA (*with a touch of hauteur*). It didn't occur to me that you could.

PETER (*very politely*). But it's only fair to warn you—that if you won't allow me to ask you certain questions tonight, then in the morning I shall take those questions to the police.

PAMELA (*alarmed, but trying to appear scornful*). My God! You must be mad.

PETER (*looking hard at* PAMELA). I'm not mad. And Diana wasn't mad.

PAMELA (*resuming her seat on the settee ; sulkily*). Her father is.

PETER (*pointedly*). Don't be too sure about that. (*He turns to* IVOR.) I've only one more question to ask you, Kemp, and then, if you don't mind, I'd like you to go out and sit in the car and wait for Mrs Fotheringham.

IVOR. Delighted. The sooner I'm out of this house—the better.

PAMELA. My sentiments exactly, Ivor darling.

PETER (*to* IVOR). Diana went straight from Barrow's house to yours, didn't she, that night?

IVOR. Yes. I know that, because she telephoned from there to me, saying she was just leaving to come over to my place.

PAMELA. That's true. I was there—and heard her.

IVOR. And between making that call and arriving at my place, there wouldn't have been time for her to go anywhere else. As it was, she must have done the journey at a hell of a lick.

PETER. Right. Well, this is the question—final one. She didn't leave several hundred pounds with you, did she?

IVOR. No, of course not. Several hundred pounds! She didn't leave ten bob for the maid.

PETER. You didn't find any money afterwards?

IVOR. No. I never find any money. I only lose it.

PETER. That's all, then. And thanks for the garage inquiry. Can you let yourself out?

IVOR. I can—and I shall enjoy it. (*He moves to the door up* R.) I'll wait for you in the car, Pam.

PAMELA. Shan't be long, darling—whatever Mr Warton may think.

IVOR. Good night then, Warton.
PETER (*moving to the door up* R.). Good night, Kemp.

(IVOR *exits up* R. PETER *closes the door, then switches off part of the lighting so that the stairs up* L. *are somewhat in shadow.*)

PAMELA. You might as well give me a drink.
PETER (*moving to the sideboard*). Certainly. What would you like? Whisky, brandy, gin?
PAMELA. Rather a lot of gin, I think, just with something to take the foul taste away. Lime or lemon, perhaps. (*She takes a cigarette case and lighter from her handbag and lights a cigarette.*)

(PETER *pours out a drink for* PAMELA.)

(*In an obviously seductive manner.*) Ivor's rather sweet, really—but quite futile, of course. I knew of course that he wasn't Diana's lover—or anybody else's—poor sweet. He wouldn't be staying with me if I didn't know he was quite harmless.

(PETER *moves to* R. *of the settee with the drink.*)

Very different from you, of course. I couldn't have *you* to stay. Or could I? (*She looks at him and takes the drink.*) Thank you. I don't think *you'd* be harmless.
PETER (*grimly*). You're right. I'm not.
PAMELA (*in the same tone as before*). Of course, poor Diana was quite fascinating—in her way. But she's dead, you know. Some of us are still alive— (*she extends a hand to* PETER) very much alive.

(PETER *ignores her outstretched hand, moves down* C., *turns and stares at her for a moment.*)

PETER. Sometimes I feel as if Diana was more alive than anybody here. I've spent so much time thinking and talking about her. Asking questions about her. Trying to understand all the different answers. She was this. She was that. She was really just an innocent child. She was a dominating unscrupulous woman. She was gentle, kind, generous, couldn't hurt anybody. She was extravagant, callous, even cruel. She was really more than half-mad. She . . .
PAMELA (*annoyed and rather alarmed*). Oh—stop it. I know all about Diana. She was one of my oldest and dearest friends. (*She pauses.*)
PETER. Go on, then. What's your version?
PAMELA. Need we talk about her?
PETER (*with a sinister inflection*). It's impossible not to talk about her in this house. There are times when I feel at any moment she'll walk into the room . . .
PAMELA (*crossly*). Oh—nonsense. You're just trying to frighten me. (*She sips her drink.*)
PETER. Go on, then, about her.

PAMELA (*carefully*). She was very attractive—could be quite fascinating in her own way—not as clever as she seemed—sometimes rather stupid—very impulsive—and unlucky.
PETER (*grimly*). She was unlucky, all right. Why did she marry Douglas Barrow?
PAMELA. One of her silly impulses. She had a row with some man she was in love with—I don't know the details, I was away then —and so to punish him—and punish herself, too—she went and married Douglas Barrow, who'd been devoted to her for years. Just one of those idiotic things women do when their emotions are all over the place. I nearly did it myself once. And that's about all I can tell you. (*She sips her drink, then places the glass on the coffee table.*)
PETER. I don't think so.
PAMELA. Well, I'll tell you this. I suspect that the man she finally meant to run away with—on the train from Longbridge Junction—was the man she had the row with before she married Douglas Barrow. I guessed that at the time. But I can't prove it.
PETER. And you wouldn't say she was mad?
PAMELA. Of course she wasn't—except that all women who're in love like that are a bit potty—poor darlings.
PETER (*quietly*). And she was a thief?
PAMELA (*startled*). Certainly not.
PETER. Well, in this room last night, Barrow said she was.
PAMELA (*contemptuously*). You didn't believe him, did you?
PETER. I believed him when he told me somebody took that Stockbreeders' Association money from his desk—nearly three hundred pounds. He certainly wasn't lying about that.
PAMELA (*uneasily*). Well—then—she must have taken it.
PETER. She asked you to go over there—and you went—and must have been there when she was packing up to go.
PAMELA. Yes, I was. She had to have *somebody* to talk to—I know just how she felt.
PETER. Did you see her take the money?
PAMELA. No, of course I didn't. But—she could have taken it before I arrived—that is, if she *did* take it.
PETER. But if she did, then what became of it? She didn't leave it with Kemp and she hadn't it when she was brought here after the accident.
PAMELA. She could have done something with it—during all that day.
PETER. Done what?
PAMELA (*impatiently*). Oh—I don't know. Hidden it somewhere. Given it to somebody.
PETER (*slowly*). It's just possible. Barrow says she must have known the money wasn't his—that he was very hard up and would have to make good the loss—which makes it a particularly mean sort of theft, doesn't it?

PAMELA (*uneasily*). Well—she wasn't like that.
PETER (*persistently*). But she must have been—if that's what she did.
PAMELA (*with uneasy impatience*). All right, then—she was. What does it matter now?
PETER (*softly*). Because she's dead?
PAMELA. Yes. And—let's face it—when you're dead—you're dead.

(LESLEY *enters quietly up* L. *and stands on the bottom stair. She looks quite unlike her usual self. She wears a very different kind of dress, of a striking type. Her hair is done loosely and very differently and she has quite a different make-up, very pale. She is, in fact, impersonating Diana.*)

PETER (*looking at* PAMELA ; *very softly*). Are you sure? (*He suddenly looks up* L. *in pretended alarm.*)

(PAMELA, *alarmed by* PETER'S *look, rises suddenly, turns, and sees* LESLEY.)

PAMELA (*screaming*). Diana! No! No! (*She collapses, half-fainting on to the settee in very real terror.*)

(PETER *glances at* PAMELA *coolly, then beckons to* LESLEY, *who moves to the fireplace, swiftly re-arranges her hair and abandons the impersonation*. PAMELA, *with her face buried in her hands, shudders and sobs.*)

PETER (*to* LESLEY). And I must say you gave me quite a shock. I didn't need to do much acting.
LESLEY (*quietly*). We were rather alike really—and this is one of her dresses, of course—it was easy. (*To* PAMELA. *Sympathetically.*) It's all right, Pamela. It's only me—Lesley.

(PAMELA *looks up, then rises in a rage.*)

PAMELA (*furiously*). My God! I could kill you for this.
PETER (*moving to* R. *of the settee ; harshly*). Sit down.
PAMELA (*with bitter hatred*). You foul brute! (*Very shakily, she resumes her seat on the settee, and sits trembling, and sobbing a little.*)
PETER (*severely*). You weren't going to tell the truth.
PAMELA. I don't know what you're talking about. And as soon as I can move at all, I'm going. Terrifying me like that.
PETER (*slowly and firmly*). If you hadn't taken that money yourself, you wouldn't have been so frightened.
LESLEY (*astonished*). Is that it?
PETER. Of course it is.
PAMELA (*angrily*). Why did you have to begin dragging everything out of everybody? It was all finished and done with. Diana died—by an accident . . .
PETER (*sharply*). No, she didn't.

PAMELA. All right, she committed suicide, then.
PETER. No, she didn't.
PAMELA (*staring at* PETER). What do you mean?
PETER (*slowly and grimly*). I think she was murdered.

(PAMELA *gives a gasp of alarm.*)

LESLEY (*urgently*). But—Peter—you said last night . . .
PETER (*interrupting; firmly*). This is something different. I think she was deliberately murdered. (*He looks severely at* PAMELA.) And now I think you might as well clear up your little part of the story. You took that money from Barrow's desk, didn't you?
PAMELA (*shakily*). Yes, I did. (*She begins to cry.*)
PETER. Go on . . .

(LESLEY *suddenly holds up her hand, checks* PETER, *and glances towards the door up* R.)

LESLEY. There's somebody at the door.
PAMELA (*wildly*). If it's Ivor, don't let him in. Don't let anybody in—for God's sake.
PETER. There's only one person who's a right to hear this—but I think it may be that person. (*He moves to the door up* R.) I asked him to look in.

(*He exits hastily up* R. PAMELA *stares at* LESLEY.)

PAMELA (*tearfully*). I don't understand. He can't let anybody in now. It's cruel—cruel. And how could you frighten me like that? Why did you do it?
LESLEY. Peter asked me to do something that might shock you into telling him the truth. I'm sorry, Pamela—but it had to come out. It seems to be much more serious than we thought—I don't understand it all myself yet—but I do know that much. And you'll have to tell the truth now.

(BARROW *and* PETER *enter up* R.)

PAMELA (*seeing* BARROW). Oh!
BARROW (*moving* C.; *astonished*). What's all this about?
PETER (*easing down* R.C.). Barrow, I think I'm right in saying that the thing that hurt you most, the thing you can't forget, is Diana taking that money.
BARROW (*gruffly*). All right, all right, Warton, we needn't go into that.
PETER. Yes, but, you see, she didn't take that money.
BARROW (*astounded*). Good God! Are you sure?
PETER (*to* PAMELA; *sympathetically*). Go on, Mrs Fotheringham. This is the one man who has a right to know—and nobody else need ever know now. But you've got to tell *him*.
PAMELA (*brokenly*). All right, I took that money, Douglas. I was desperate. It was—just before Wilfred was killed—I was expecting

him home on leave—and I didn't know what to do—I'd been spending too much and I was terrified of what he'd say. I was always afraid of Wilfred really particularly about money. (*She looks up at* BARROW. *With an effort*.) I saw it lying there, while Diana was finishing packing upstairs. I didn't know it wasn't yours. I didn't know you were hard up. I swear I didn't. I always thought that between you, you and Diana had plenty of money. She was leaving you. It might have been her money. She was always careless. So I took it—stuffed some of it in my bag and some in my coat pockets. I'd have paid it back afterwards—but Diana was dead—and you went away—and it seemed to be all over and done with. Don't look at me like that, Douglas—please. I'm desperately sorry—and I've suffered, too. And I'll pay you back—every penny. (*She looks hopefully at* BARROW.)

BARROW (*slowly*). It isn't the money—though I could do with it now.

PAMELA (*eagerly*). You shall have it, I promise.

BARROW (*slowly*). It's what I thought about Diana. And I was wrong all the time.

PETER (*quietly*). Yes, you were wrong all the time. Wrong about Kemp, too. And it was the man she was originally in love with—before she married you—the man she never stopped being in love with that she ran away to join.

BARROW (*slowly*). I see. And it makes a hell of a difference—when you come to think about it—doesn't it?

PAMELA (*still rather brokenly*). Douglas please! It's better for you now make it better for me. I don't care if I'm talking like a crazy kid—I can't help it—but say you forgive me.

BARROW. All right, let's forget it—when you've paid up.

PAMELA (*eagerly*). Yes—of course.

BARROW (*gruff, but friendly*). I'll take you out to your car. (*He turns to* PETER.) No point in either of us staying, is there?

PETER. No. I just wanted you to learn that Diana hadn't taken that money.

(PAMELA *pulls herself together*.)

BARROW. Much obliged, Warton. (*He looks down at* PAMELA *and holds out a hand to help her to rise*.) Come on, then, Pamela. Let's go somewhere where we don't look such dam' fools. (*He pulls* PAMELA *to her feet, then steadies her and leads her to the door up* R.)

(PETER *moves to the door up* R. *and opens it*.)

Steady the Buffs! No need to cry. All over now. Here we go. 'Night, Miss Dereham. (*As he goes*.) Let ourselves out—don't bother, old boy. 'Night, Warton. 'Night. 'Night.

(*He exits with* PAMELA *up* R. PETER *stands watching them off for a moment, then closes the door and moves* C.)

LESLEY (*sitting on the settee*). He was rather sweet with her as he took her out, wasn't he? She's a widow, and he's a widower—perhaps something will come of it.

PETER (*crossing to the fireplace*). And then they can keep that three hundred pounds in the family.

LESLEY. I'm glad Diana didn't take it. But why did you think it so important to prove she didn't?

PETER. Various reasons. I was sorry for Barrow. I wanted to get the truth, and that didn't sound like the truth. And then you may remember that before the Major told us his story last night, when you asked him what could have become of all that money, he said " Anything. She may have thrown it away." That fitted in nicely with what he was about to tell us—that she was really off her head.

LESLEY (*eagerly*). And now we know that everything she did during those two days was quite reasonable. Though I think going to Ivor Kemp was rather silly.

PETER. She had to fill in a day somewhere, and she didn't want to come back here and didn't want to leave the district. And she wasn't above using poor Kemp as a stooge, so nobody would suspect the real man.

LESLEY (*dryly*). You know quite a lot about it, don't you?

PETER. I'm learning.

LESLEY. Or—remembering.

PETER. I said—learning.

LESLEY. I heard you. But, you see, there's that other man, the real one, the one she was going off with. When are you going to tell me about him?

PETER. Any time you like now.

LESLEY. I don't think I want to know.

PETER. You've got it all wrong, you know.

LESLEY (*angrily*). Everybody here's been wrong about everything connected with Diana except you, haven't they?

PETER (*coolly*). Nearly—but not quite.

LESLEY (*exasperated*). Oh! You . . .

PETER (*hushing her*). Listen! (*He crosses quickly to the door up* R., *opens it softly, glances off, then closes the door and turns.*) Your uncle's coming down.

LESLEY (*rising hurriedly*). I must take this beastly dress off.

(*She exits quickly up* L. PETER *crosses to the fireplace. After a moment the* COLONEL *enters up* R. *He wears a thick dressing-gown and slippers.*)

COLONEL (*moving to the settee*). Ah—so you're back, Warton?

PETER. Been back some time, sir.

COLONEL (*sitting heavily on the settee*). I couldn't sleep. That's one bad result of following your instructions, my boy, and not taking George's medicine.

PETER. I'm sorry—but . . .

COLONEL (*shakily*). No, you were quite right. My mind's much clearer now—though I'm still bewildered. I'm an old man, Warton —and so much has happened—and it's difficult. (*He pauses.*) But —will you tell me the truth?

PETER. Yes, sir. That's what I want to do.

COLONEL. My daughter died, didn't she?

PETER (*quietly*). Yes, sir.

COLONEL (*sadly*). I think I knew, in a way, all the time. There was no deliberate pretence—I was all confused—you're too young to understand—but somewhere—at the back of my mind—I knew. (*He pauses.*) Do you know how she died?

PETER (*slowly*). I think I do—now.

COLONEL. Tell me the truth—did I—did I—kill her?

PETER. No, you didn't, Colonel Risborough.

COLONEL. But—she didn't die a natural death—there was something wrong   some mystery.

PETER (*softly*). Yes, there was a mystery that I came here to try to solve.

COLONEL. She—killed herself, then? It's hard to believe that —a girl so full of life—with so much . . .

PETER. I don't think she killed herself.

COLONEL (*eagerly*). An accident, perhaps?

PETER. An accident? (*He is about to dismiss this, when he suddenly checks himself and looks speculatively at the* COLONEL.) Yes, I suppose it could have been an accident.

COLONEL (*eagerly*). She'd never have done it deliberately. Not that sort at all. High-spirited—reckless sometimes—always inclined to overdo everything—but no suicide. Eh, Warton? I'm counting on you to back me up here—to set my mind at rest.

PETER (*uncertainly*). I'll do what I can.

COLONEL. Well, what have you found out? What can you prove? That it was an accident?

PETER (*slowly*). I know that she had a good reason for coming here that night, and that she had no intention of committing suicide. There was no reason why she should.

COLONEL (*eagerly*). Then it must have been an accident, then—eh?

PETER (*slowly*). It must have been some sort of accident.

(*The* MAJOR *enters up* L. *He wears pyjamas, dressing-gown and slippers. He smokes his pipe, and looks a cosy old fellow. He stares at the* COLONEL *and* PETER *for a moment, then moves* C.)

MAJOR. Now what's all this?

COLONEL. Well, George, I might as well admit it. I've been stealing a march on you. Dropped your medicine for the last day or two—it was much too strong, George, though I'm not blaming you —and I've been plotting with young Warton here.

MAJOR (*comfortably*). What about? (*He moves to the sideboard.*) Anybody else want a drink? (*He starts to pour out a drink for himself.*)

COLONEL (*shakily, but with enthusiasm*). We've got the whole thing all wrong. I mean, about Diana. It was an accident. And I believe Warton can prove it. Can't you, my boy?

(*As the* COLONEL *looks at* WARTON, *he and the* MAJOR *look at each other. Then the* MAJOR *turns again to attend to his drink.*)

PETER. I can prove some things.

MAJOR (*moving down* C.). Done some successful sleuthing, have you? (*He lifts his glass.*) Cheers! (*He drinks.*)

PETER. Yes, it hasn't worked out badly.

MAJOR. You surprise me.

PETER. Beginner's luck, perhaps.

MAJOR (*half jocularly*). But you persuaded the Colonel to deceive his medical adviser—and one of his oldest friends—eh?

PETER. Well . . .

COLONEL (*interrupting*). Allow me to answer that, Warton. It was just a little notion we had, George, that perhaps this stuff you were giving me might be stronger than you thought, and doing me more harm than good.

MAJOR. Would I want to do you more harm than good, Philip?

COLONEL (*heartily*). Of course not, my dear fellow. Idea never entered my head. But—well, you're getting on, George—out of touch a bit—out of practice.

MAJOR (*sadly*). I suppose so—though I hate admitting it.

COLONEL (*rising and moving to the* MAJOR ; *heartily*). Now, now, old boy—mustn't take it like that. (*He shakes the* MAJOR *by the hand.*) And no harm done at all. Believe I might try and sleep now.

(LESLEY *enters up* L. *She has changed her dress.*)

MAJOR. A mild hot drink might help.

LESLEY (*moving above the settee*). I want something, too—hot and milky—so shall I bring you something, Uncle?

COLONEL. Very good of you, my dear. (*He moves slowly to the door up* R.) It was all an accident, y'know—about poor Diana. Might have happened to anybody. But we'll talk about that tomorrow. 'Night, George. 'Night, Warton.

(*He exits up* R. LESLEY *moves to follow him, but looks enquiringly at* PETER.)

PETER (*moving up* C.). You attend to your hot drinks, please, Lesley.

LESLEY. Will you two—be all right?

MAJOR (*heartily*). Why not?

PETER (*dryly*). Why not?

(LESLEY *gives them one last wondering look, then exits up* R. *The* MAJOR *moves to the settee, sits, puts his glass on the coffee table, relights his pipe and looks cosy.* PETER *eases down* C.)

MAJOR. Well—Warton ?
PETER (*quickly*). You killed her.
MAJOR (*easily*). My dear chap, don't be ridiculous. I told you last night what happened.
PETER. Yes, but I didn't believe a word of it.
MAJOR. Why not ?
PETER. Well, to begin with, you told us you found the Colonel in Diana's room at midnight. But Mrs Probus told me she heard the Colonel snoring heavily, like a man in heavily drugged sleep, just after midnight.
MAJOR. She might by lying, you know.
PETER. I don't think so. And her little bit of evidence, among other things, puts your story where it belongs—in the dustbin.
MAJOR. You'll have to do better than that, Warton.
PETER. All right. How about this ? Your story was based on the idea, which you thought we'd sold ourselves, that everything Diana did those last two days was unreasonable, idiotic—she was off her head, you see. But now we know that isn't the case.
MAJOR. What about the money she stole and then threw away—for instance ?
PETER. She didn't take that money. So you'll have to do better than that, too. In fact, a lot better. You see, last night you overcalled your hand—too confident. There wasn't the slightest reason to tell that story last night if *it were true*. If you'd been the man in that story covering up for an old friend, then *you wouldn't have told it*.
MAJOR. Nonsense ! I told it so that you would stop this investigation of yours, which couldn't do any of us any good.
PETER. But if what you told us last night was true, then the worst that could have happened from my investigation would have been my discovery that the Colonel killed her. So to prevent the worst happening, you went and gave it to us on a plate. No, Major. It was a bad move. All wrong. I guessed at once that you'd invented that story to hide something much worse, from your point of view, and as a bold bid to stop me from discovering what that something was. So there it is. Diana wasn't off her head. The Colonel wasn't in her room when you said he was. And you invented that story to stop me from finding out anything else.
MAJOR. All right, Warton. I'll be frank with you. What I told you last night wasn't true. And I merely pretended it was to stop you continuing this investigation of yours. But really I told that story for Lesley and not for you.
PETER. Why Lesley ?
MAJOR. Because I wanted to make sure of staying on here. You

see, I'm being perfectly frank with you now. I don't want to leave this place. And last night seemed to me a good opportunity to explain Diana's death so that Lesley, who doesn't like me much, would be as anxious as I am for me to stay on here.

PETER. Like that, eh?

MAJOR. Like that. Not very creditable, perhaps—but I'm getting on, and I'm a poor man and I like my comforts.

PETER. And Diana?

MAJOR (*confidently*). No mystery about that, my dear chap. Diana killed herself, of course. She'd gone to meet her lover, the night before, and he hadn't turned up—and after that she didn't care—nothing to live for.

PETER. You sure?

MAJOR. Of course. She admitted as much.

PETER. And that's just one lie too many, Major. Diana didn't find her chap at Longbridge Junction, not because he let her down but because she missed the train. She knew he had to catch it because he was on duty and had to report up North the next morning. And as soon as she'd recovered from her accident, she'd have followed him up North. But *you didn't know that, Major.* You thought she'd come home for good. And that's why you killed her.

MAJOR. This is idiotic, Warton. What motive had I?

PETER. You've just told me. Getting on—a poor man—and you like your comforts. You'd made up your mind that whatever happened, you'd never return to that little bed-sitting room in a dingy back street. You didn't like Diana, and you knew she didn't like you. If she stayed on here, it was all up with you. But if she was out of the way, not only could you stay on here, but you had a good chance of being left a nice large slice of the Colonel's money. And he wouldn't last too long if you kept him half-doped. You'd given him a large dose that night you killed her, and that's why Mrs Probus heard him sleeping so heavily. You shouldn't have overlooked Mrs Probus. You oughtn't to have let me see Mrs Fotheringham, Barrow and Kemp, and go to Longbridge Junction. You shouldn't have overplayed your hand last night. And once you'd told that story, you should have stuck to it. And you ought to have kept a better eye on the Colonel these last two days. You've grown careless, Major. And now I know—you killed her.

MAJOR. I'm afraid I seriously under-rated your intelligence, my dear fellow. Particularly stupid of me, if only because I've depended to a large extent on people under-rating *my* intelligence—you know, retired major—silly old buffer. (*He picks up his glass and drinks.*) I ought to have known better. (*He rises.*) Join me in a drink? (*He moves to the sideboard.*)

PETER. I think I will, now. (*He moves to the sideboard.*)

(*They each pour out their own drinks.*)

But I haven't changed the subject, you know. It's still *murder*.
(*He moves to the easy chair* C. *and sits*.)
    MAJOR (*moving to the settee*). Just as you like. (*He raises his glass*.) Cheers ! (*He drinks*.)
    PETER. Cheers ! (*He drinks*.)
    MAJOR (*sitting on the settee*). Now let's suppose, just for the sake of argument, that I did kill this wretched girl. What are you going to do about it ?
    PETER. I don't know yet.
    MAJOR. You don't know how I did it. And you can never produce a witness. Even the motive—although I agree with you that actually it's a very strong one—would look flimsy and ridiculous in court. Any competent defending counsel would blow your case to bits in five minutes. In the meantime, the whole messy business, involving half-a-dozen people who've had more than enough of it already, is dragged into the limelight. Look at my poor old friend, the Colonel. Now that he thinks it was an accident, he's better and brighter than I've seen him for months. But now you'd like to stick him in the witness box, poor old boy, to try to prove that one of his oldest friends killed his daughter.
    PETER. I've already thought of that. By the way, just for my own satisfaction, you did kill her, didn't you ?

(*Unseen by* PETER *and the* MAJOR, LESLEY *enters quietly up* L., *and stands on the bottom stair listening*.)

    MAJOR. Well, just between ourselves—and of course I'd deny it in any other company—I did kill her. Nothing painful and brutal. A strong sedative—and then—a pillow. No trouble at all. Just between ourselves, of course.
    LESLEY (*suddenly*). No, it isn't.

(PETER *and the* MAJOR *turn, startled*.)

(*With sudden emotion*.) Oh—it's horrible. And how you can sit there, both of you, talking so calmly . . . (*She starts to cry a little*.)
    PETER (*rising quickly and moving to* LESLEY). All right, Lesley. Take it easy. (*He leads her to the easy chair down* R.) How much did you overhear ?
    LESLEY (*sitting ; her voice muffled by her handkerchief*). Everything he said. I daren't interrupt you.
    PETER. All right, my dear. Quiet now. We've got to think. (*He turns to the* MAJOR.) Our case looks a bit stronger now, doesn't it ?
    MAJOR. A little—but—a young man from nowhere—an infatuated hysterical girl— (*to* LESLEY) I'm sorry, my dear, but that's how I should describe you, speaking as a medical man, too— (*to* PETER) wild talk at midnight— (*he shrugs his shoulders*) I doubt if this makes much difference. And most of my arguments still apply. Think of the Colonel, for instance.

LESLEY. Peter, he's right about uncle Philip. We can't drag him into this.
PETER. I know. He's had enough, poor old boy. (*He pauses.*) Has he any other old regimental chum who could stay with him here?
MAJOR. There's Major Jeffers, who's situated more or less as I was. He's a bore and not quite a gentleman—but the Colonel doesn't mind having him around. Why?
PETER. I want to get back to my job as soon as I can fly next week, if possible. Major Buttershaw, I'll give you exactly forty-eight hours to take yourself out of this, for good, and to get this other fellow—Jeffers—here. If you refuse, I'm going to the police with the whole story.
LESLEY. And I'll go with him.

(*There is a pause.* LESLEY *and* PETER *look at the* MAJOR, *who is cool and smiling.*)

MAJOR. Play poker at all, Warton?
PETER. Yes.
MAJOR. I used to—in the old days.
PETER. And you think I'm bluffing when I say I'll take my story to the police?
MAJOR (*smiling*). Yes. And I'm calling your bluff.
PETER (*decisively*). Right. That's all I wanted to know. (*He moves to the desk, puts his glass on it and refers to the telephone directory.*)

(LESLEY *rises and breaks down* R. *The* MAJOR *rises and moves up* C. *They both watch* PETER *intently as he lifts the receiver and dials a number. The* MAJOR *takes out his handkerchief and anxiously dabs at his forehead.*)

(*Into the telephone.*) Hello—is that the County Police?
MAJOR (*urgently*). No, Warton, drop it.

(PETER *looks enquiringly at the* MAJOR.)

You win. (*He drains his glass and puts it on the sideboard.*)
PETER (*into the telephone*). Sorry—all a mistake. (*He replaces the receiver and turns to the* MAJOR. *Severely.*) Forty-eight hours. And no tricks.
MAJOR (*shrugging his shoulders*). I'm too old—too tired. Mind if I take the decanter? (*He picks up the decanter from the sideboard, moves up* L. *and turns.*) But I still think she'd never have been any good to anybody. You were well out of that, Warton. Young Lesley there is worth ten of her. 'Night.

(*He turns and exits up* L. *There is a pause.*)

LESLEY. It was the only thing to do, I suppose—to let him go like that.

PETER (*moving* C.). Yes, we could never have proved it. And anyhow—he's finished, and we had to think of your uncle.

LESLEY (*easing* R.C.). Yes. Are you really going back to Burma next week?

PETER. Probably. Come with me.

LESLEY. Why should I?

PETER. Because I want you to. And you'd like it there. Lovely place. Plenty of sun, flowers, fruit, golden temples, fun and games.

(LESLEY *shakes her head wistfully*.)

What does that mean?

LESLEY. It wouldn't work. I've thought about it—oh, I won't pretend I haven't—but I know it wouldn't work.

PETER. Why not?

LESLEY. Don't you see there'd always be a shadow between us—Diana? Yes—and the worst kind—a bright shadow. What's the use? You were in love with her. That's why you came back here. And deep down you'll always be in love with her—and I shall know it. Poor Diana—there wasn't really anything specially mysterious and elusive about her. I know what she was like—after all, she was my cousin. An ordinary sort of girl—impulsive—and rather silly and empty. But it's no use telling you that. You'll always remember her as you saw her here—lovely and gay. And you can't forget her.

PETER. Can't I?

LESLEY. No, I proved that.

PETER. How?

LESLEY. When I came down tonight, looking like her. Pamela had known her for years, but for a moment she thought it was really Diana. But you didn't. You weren't deceived for a second. Simply because—being still in love with her—you remembered her even better than Pamela did. So she'd always stand between us—don't you see?

PETER (*smiling*). The bright shadow.

LESLEY (*sadly*). The bright shadow.

PETER (*moving to* L. *of* LESLEY). You know, it's about time I started kissing you.

LESLEY. No—no. I want you to. But not when you're going—and I know it wouldn't work between us.

PETER (*holding her at arm's length*). Now let me tell you something. You've got everything the wrong way round. There was a very good reason why I didn't recognize you as Diana. You see, I'd never set eyes on Diana.

LESLEY (*astounded*). What? But—Peter . . .

PETER (*interrupting*). I never set eyes on Diana. I never came to this house during the war. I was never within miles of the place. And you ought to have spotted that—it was obvious.

LESLEY. But why did you come here now?

PETER. I have a partner out in Burma—a bloke called Hubert Sheraton, who was a Wing-Commander stationed at Dillingley.

LESLEY. And was he the man . . . ?

PETER (*interrupting*). He was the man Diana fell in love with, had the row with, and then missed that night at Longbridge Junction. They had to be careful because he was just divorcing his wife. When Diana wasn't at the station, he thought she'd changed her mind again—and then, of course, soon afterwards, he learnt that she was dead. And ever since, she's been haunting him—your bright shadow and so I promised, as I was coming over here, to find out for him what really happened. I want a partner with his mind on the business.

LESLEY. Then I want our minds on our business. Kiss me.

(PETER *takes her in his arms and kisses her with enthusiasm*.)

(*She disengages herself*.) What did you say it was like in Burma?

PETER (*grinning*). Hot as blazes, rains like hell, snakes, spiders, flies, all work and no money.

LESLEY. Right. When do we go?

QUICK CURTAIN

FURNITURE AND PROPERTY LIST.

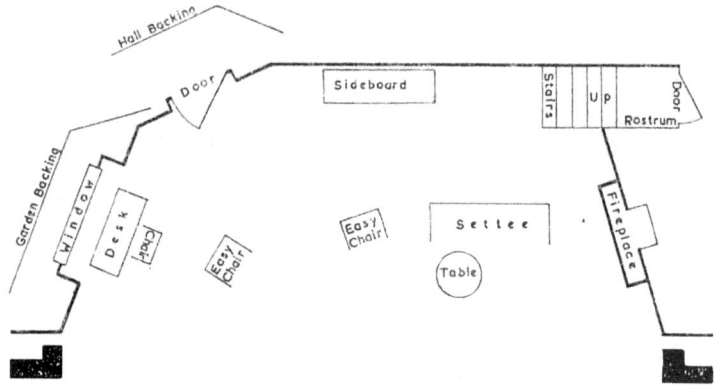

Throughout the play :
On Stage.

    Settee. *On it* : cushions.

    2 Easy chairs. *On them* : cushions.

    Desk. *On it* : blotter, inkstand, pens, telephone, telephone directory, ashtray.

    Sideboard. *On it* : decanter of whisky, syphon of soda, box of cigarettes, matches, ashtray, bottles of gin, vermouth, sherry, lime, and brandy, jug of water, glasses.

    Coffee table.

    Desk chair.

    Standard lamps.

    Pictures on wall.

    Carpet.

    Curtains at window.

    Fire-irons.

    Hearth-rug.

    On mantelpiece : ornaments, ashtray.

ACT I.

Set.—*On coffee table* : 3 cups, 3 saucers, 3 teaspoons, teapot, sugar basin, milk jug, 3 plates, plate of scones.

Off Stage.

    Tray (MRS PROBUS).

    Peter's hat and overcoat (MRS PROBUS).

    Suitcase (COLONEL).

Personal.
PAMELA : wrist watch
MAJOR : pipe, matches, pouch with tobacco.
LESLEY : scarf.
Curtains open.
Fire on.
Standard lamps off.

ACT II.

Strike.
LESLEY'S scarf.
Dirty glasses.
Suitcase, hat and raincoat.

Set.—*On coffee table :* tray with 4 coffee cups, 4 saucers, 4 spoons, coffee pot, sugar basin, milk jug.

Personal.
PETER : case with cigarettes, lighter, note-book, pencil, handkerchief.
MAJOR : pipe, matches.
LESLEY : handkerchief.
Curtains closed.
Fire on.
Standard lamps on.

ACT III.

Strike.—Dirty glasses.

Set.
On coffee table : tray with 4 coffee cups, 4 saucers, 4 spoons, coffee pot, sugar basin, milk jug.
On settee : sewing for Lesley.
On easy chair R.C. : copy of *The Times.*

Personal.
MAJOR : pipe, matches, pocket-watch, handkerchief.
PETER : wallet. *In it :* 3 10s. notes.
PAMELA : handbag. *In it :* case with cigarettes, lighter, handkerchief.
LESLEY : handkerchief.
Curtains closed.
Fire on.
Standard lamps on.

LIGHTING PLOT.

ACT I.

To open:
All lights checked to $\frac{1}{2}$.
Late sunlight through window.
Standard lamps off.
Fire on.

At rise: Start slow fade of sunlight to $\frac{1}{4}$.
At cue.—LESLEY switches on lights—all lights up to full, standard lamps on.

ACT II.

To open.
All lights checked to $\frac{3}{4}$.
Standard lamps on.
Fire on.
No cues.

ACT III.

To open.
All lights full up.
Standard lamps on.
Fire on.
At cue.—PETER switches off light—check lights to $\frac{1}{2}$.